Allen Iverson: The Inspiring Story of One of Basketball's Greatest Shooting Guards

An Unauthorized Biography

By: Clayton Geoffreys

Table of Contents

Foreword

Entering the new millennium, few players had as much of an influence on the game of basketball as Allen Iverson. Known for his infamous crossover, Iverson was one the original score-first guards of the 21st century. Slashing and dashing his way through the lane, Allen Iverson entertained not only the city of Philadelphia, but also the entire audience of the NBA. Yet, despite his accomplishments, Allen Iverson never won an NBA title in his time playing in the league, and his legacy is and continues to be often scrutinized due to his personality traits. Regardless of what others think, Allen Iverson always did it his way, from the very beginning of when he first entered the NBA until the very end when his career abruptly came to an end. Thank you for downloading *Allen Iverson: The Incredible Story of One of Basketball's Greatest Shooting Guards*. In this unauthorized biography, we will learn Allen Iverson's incredible life story and impact on the game of basketball. Hope you enjoy and if you do, please do not forget to leave a review!

Also, check out my website at claytongeoffreys.com to join my exclusive list where I let you know about my latest books and give you goodies!

Cheers,

Clayton Geoffreys

Visit me at www.claytongeoffreys.com

Introduction

To discuss Allen Iverson is to examine the importance of narratives in basketball. No NBA player's legacy has been so starkly divided between those who hail Iverson and those who disdain him. After all, he is still regarded as one of the more polarizing figures the league has ever seen.

On one side, Allen Iverson is considered as a fearsome, relentless warrior. Despite subpar supporting casts throughout his career, he fought and bled for victory every single game. He had an unparalleled will to win and inspired fanatical loyalty in his teammates. He struggled through hardships, poverty, and his size not just to reach the NBA but to become one of the best players of all time.

Regarded as perhaps the greatest player pound for pound, Allen Iverson was barely 6 feet tall but had the heart of a lion. He never cared about his size or who was defending and meeting him at the basket. All he cared about was that he made the baskets that he wanted to score. All he cared about was fighting through the adversity that came with his size and the criticisms that came with his attitude and spunk as an NBA player.

In one of the greatest performances in NBA history, Allen Iverson stole Game 1 of the NBA Finals against one of the greatest NBA teams ever, the 2001 Los Angeles Lakers. It was the only defeat that Los Angeles had on their road to the 2001 championship. It was that victory that epitomized Iverson's heart and will. He won the MVP award in 2001 for an average of 30 points per game year in and year out. He is without a doubt the greatest little man in NBA history.

On the other side, Allen Iverson was regarded a selfish and arrogant team-killer. The subpar supporting casts were, in fact, a perfect fit for his talents. Iverson's determination only showed when he could dominate the ball as much as he liked, and he promptly threw temper tantrums otherwise. That 2001 MVP should have gone to eventual Finals MVP Shaquille O'Neal, and while that Game 1 performance was impressive, the reality is that the 2001 Philadelphia 76ers squad would have never made it to the NBA Finals if they had not played in a miserable Eastern Conference. He scored many points, but with his flaws and temperament, he was utterly incapable of playing on a championship team.

Nobody saw Allen Iverson as a team player, either. He always wanted the ball in his hands. The possessions started and ended with him. While initially in his career nobody could question why he had to take 90% of the shots for his team, it was his partnership with Carmelo Anthony later when he moved over to the Denver Nuggets that solidified criticisms about his willingness to share the ball.

Both Iverson and Anthony are regarded as two great scorers that needed the ball as much as possible in isolation situations. It was a partnership that was predicated on taking turns. On one play, it was AI, and on the next one, it was Melo. While Iverson had the luxury of playing with another superstar at that point in his career, it was clear that he was better off as a one-man show. The Denver Nuggets never got far with him pairing up with the prolific scoring forward.

The decision of which interpretation of Iverson is correct is for history to decide. But for fourteen NBA seasons, Allen Iverson electrified the hearts of NBA fans around the world. Iverson was the player whom every child at the local basketball court wanted to be. He carried himself on the court with a relentless bravado unmatched by anyone. With his flashy sense of style, he inspired a fashion revolution and created a synthesis between basketball and hip-hop which lasted even after his departure from the NBA. Even his sudden collapse when he went from being a legitimate All-Star in 2008 to out of the NBA by 2010 inspired pathos and awe. Until he formally retired in 2013, fans and sportswriters wondered whether he would ever return to the NBA.

Iverson may not have been the best player or leader, and his career may have ended without a bang but with a whimper, but in the eyes of many, his drive and determination exhibited just how exciting and thrilling the NBA could be. After Iverson's retirement, All-NBA point guard Chris Paul said that Iverson had a bigger influence on basketball than Michael Jordan and that his imprint on basketball would never be forgotten. That statement showed just how valuable Iverson was to the game.

Chapter 1: Childhood and Early Life

Allen Ezail Iverson was born on June 7, 1975, in Hampton, Virginia. His mother, Ann Iverson, was then just fifteen years old. Allen's father left his mother after he was born and Ann was left to care for her newborn son alone. Consequently, Ann dropped out of high school and moved in with her mother. Until the Iversons and Ann's new partner, Michael Freeman, moved into an apartment when Allen was 7, the young Allen lived with 13 other people in his grandmother's house.

Young Iverson's childhood was incredibly difficult. He grew up without reliable electricity or running water. At one point, raw sewage even leaked into the house so badly that everyone inside had to wear boots for safety. Although Ann could have hated her son for drastically changing her life, she did nothing of the sort. She raised Allen as well she could and encouraged her son that he could go far and reach his dreams if he worked hard enough.

Fortunately for the family, Allen Iverson was born with incredible athletic talent. When Ann saw her 22-inch baby with hands past his knees for the first time, she cried out, "He gonna be a ball player!" Although he would eventually have a Hall of Fame NBA career, Iverson started out by playing football more than basketball. In fact, he was attracted to football almost as soon as he could walk. When he was four years old, "Bubbachuck," as Allen was known in Hampton, was already playing tackle football with older boys. Iverson was faster and agiler than his opponents, and that was not his only advantage. No matter how often or how hard he was slammed and hit by his bigger playmates, Allen would get right back up and attack again. Allen Iverson loved football and initially disdained basketball, perceiving the latter as a soft sport.

But Ann had other ideas. Ann believed that sports would be the only way for Allen to escape the drug and crime-riddled streets of Hampton, so she forced Iverson to play basketball alongside football. She held off paying the electricity bill to enroll her son in a basketball camp and to give him new Air Jordan shoes. Iverson refused to attend the camp at first, but Ann responded by telling him that he would not enter her house until he went to the camp. Iverson cursed his mother every step of the way there, but upon arriving, he realized that he was far more athletic and talented than everyone else there. When he returned from training camp, he thanked his mother for her sacrifice.

Iverson continued to play both basketball and football, showing off his incredible talents. However, as early as middle school, Iverson already established a reputation for being a high-maintenance player. He repeatedly cut classes and argued with his teachers and coaches. He was nearly not invited to a national Amateur Athletic Union (AAU) 13-and-under tournament because of his reputation. Iverson eventually did go, and his team placed second in the country. On the way back home, the rest of the team celebrated, but Iverson tossed the second place trophy out of the window. He declared that he was not interested in second place. It was a personality trait that stuck with Iverson his entire life.

Chapter 2: High School Years

Iverson attended Bethel High School in Virginia. However, right after he enrolled, tragedy struck. His stepfather, Michael Freeman, was caught selling cocaine and was imprisoned. Without Freeman's income as a naval yard worker, the Iversons were forcibly evicted from their apartment in Iverson's sophomore year. Ann moved to a shelter and decided to have Allen live with family friend, Gary Moore. Moore had coached Allen in youth football and was determined to make sure that he did not go down the wrong path. With further assistance from Iverson's coach, Mike Bailey, Iverson managed to get satisfactory grades and stay out of trouble in his early years in high school.

Iverson quickly became one of the most dominant high school athletes in the country, and football continued to be his favorite sport. His primary position was quarterback, and he showed real passing ability, but he also played running back, kick returner, and defensive back. In Iverson's junior year, he led Bethel High to the Virginia state football championships. Iverson declared in the postgame interview that he also wanted to lead Bethel High to the basketball championship, which he did as well. As a result, he received the Associated Press Player of the Year in both sports.

As a high school basketball player, Iverson was a sensation. Bethel High School had to move their basketball games out of their regular gym because so many people wanted to see the small point guard do whatever he pleased on the court. In Iverson's junior year, he scored 948 points just for the season, setting a Virginia high school record that stands to this day. His crossovers devastated high school players just as it would NBA players and Iverson regularly dunked on his bigger opponents. However, he did have problems with his temper and cut a staggering number of classes. Nevertheless, he was one of the top basketball and football prospects in the country and seemed to be well on his way to making it to college.

But in one night, all of those dreams nearly turned to dust. On February 14, 1993, Iverson was at a local bowling alley when a melee broke out between Iverson's black friends and a group of whites. Chairs were flung, and three people landed in the emergency room, including a white woman. A week after the brawl, Allen Iverson and three of his friends were arrested. According to certain witnesses, Iverson had thrown the chair that hit the white woman, Barbara Steele. Iverson denied the allegations and declared that he had not even thrown a single punch, much less a chair. Nevertheless, Iverson was charged; not with assault, but with "maiming by mob," a Virginia statute passed during the Reconstruction to prevent the lynching of blacks. With the maiming by mob charge, the prosecution would not need to prove that Iverson had flung the chair that hurt Ms. Steele. All they had to prove was that Iverson was in fact at the brawl. Iverson was eventually proven guilty. Most people expected a slap on the wrist and some form of community service or probation. Instead, Iverson was shockingly sentenced to 5 years in prison, with the possibility of release in 10 months provided he had good behavior.

The local blacks in Hampton were enraged by Iverson's sentence. They believed that various aspects of the trial, such as questionable moves by the defense and the judge's record, were marred by racism and that Iverson was innocent. Large sections of the black community vehemently protested for Iverson to be set free. Even national voices, like Tom Brokaw and Sports Illustrated, lent their voices to the debate. Iverson himself admitted to Brokaw that he somewhat resented all of the attention. At the minimum-security Newport News City Farm prison, Iverson worked at the bakery and continued to shoot baskets by himself. In December 1993, Douglas Wilder, the first black governor in the history of Virginia, pardoned Iverson as well as his three friends after serving only four months in prison. Later, in 1995, Iverson's conviction was overturned due to lack of evidence, removing his record as an ex-felon.

Although Iverson was now a free man, his conviction still lingered over him and limited his options. He missed what would have been his senior year's football season. In fact, he had no senior year at that point as he was no longer allowed to attend Bethel High. Iverson, however, still managed to complete his high school education with the help of a private tutor, Sue Lambiotte. Iverson had not played organized basketball or football ever since he went to prison. Colleges that would have offered him a scholarship looked elsewhere, fearful of Iverson's temperament and any possible adverse publicity.

Desperate to get her son into college and away from Hampton, Ann met with Georgetown University basketball coach, John Thompson, and begged him to give Allen a chance. Although wary, Thompson met with Allen, and he was impressed by Iverson's intelligence and believed that Iverson's time in prison was behind him. In April 1994, Iverson received a full basketball scholarship to Georgetown. Little Bubbachuck had finally managed to make it to college. His dreams of football dominance may have died in that bowling alley, but Iverson might still have a chance to make it into the NBA.

Chapter 3: College Years at Georgetown

From the moment Iverson stepped onto the Georgetown Hoyas court, it was clear that his time away from basketball had not hampered his athletic skills. In his first exhibition game against Fort Hood, Iverson scored 36 points along with five assists and three steals in just 23 minutes. Georgetown has traditionally been a school for great college big men with alumni like NBA All-Stars Patrick Ewing, Alonzo Mourning, and Dikembe Mutombo. Coach Thompson had initially planned to use Iverson as a sixth man, but Iverson was so powerful, fast, and skilled that Thompson made him the focus of the team. Iverson routinely scored 20 to 30 points night in and night out, such as a 31-point performance against DePaul and 30 against Providence. Georgetown had a 21-10 record in Iverson's freshman year and qualified for the NCAA tournament.

But that did not mean that all was well for the Hoyas. It was at Georgetown that the allegations of Iverson being a ball hog first appeared. Iverson turned the ball over nearly as often as he passed it for the assist. At times, he would attempt shots that made little sense, and Thompson, as well as Iverson's teammates, grew frustrated with how much he dominated the ball. In the 1995 NCAA tournament, Georgetown would reach the Sweet 16 before being eliminated by North Carolina and their duo of future NBA stars, Jerry Stackhouse and Rasheed Wallace.

Although Georgetown had gone further in this year's tournament than in the 1994 NCAA tournament, Iverson played a minimal role in Georgetown's two wins over Xavier and Weber State. He scored just 32 points combined in those two games and took 37 shots in the process. Iverson averaged 20 points per game as a freshman and was named the Big East Rookie of the Year, the Big East Defensive Player of the Year, and the All-Rookie Tournament First Team. However, Iverson knew that if he wanted to earn a high NBA draft selection, he would have to show that he could function as a point guard.

In his sophomore year, Iverson developed a great deal. His scoring improved to 25 points a game and became far more efficient as well. Iverson developed his shooting touch as well as his tendency to take bad shots. His field goal percentage leaped from 39% to 48% and his three-point shooting went from 23% to 36%. Iverson also let his teammates handle the ball more, which decreased his turnovers from 4.4 to 3.8 a game.

But even if his teammates had the ball more now, none of them could take over a basketball game like Iverson. He scored 40 points twice over the NCAA season and regularly dropped more than 30 points with excellent efficiency. In a match against the rival Connecticut Huskies, Iverson went up against future All-Star shooting guard, Ray Allen. Iverson outplayed Ray Allen by grabbing 26 points, eight steals, and six assists, and punctuated Georgetown's 77-65 victory with a dunk in Ray Allen's face. Georgetown finished the regular season with an impressive 29-8 record and was viewed as a legitimate contender for the Final Four. After winning their first three games of the NCAA tournament, Georgetown faced off against Massachusetts, led by defensive center, Marcus Camby. Massachusetts was the favorite, and Camby was just too much for Georgetown's big men to handle. Camby scored 22 points while Iverson had a disappointing 6 out of 21 shooting performance. Massachusetts crushed Georgetown, 86-62. Even though Georgetown had failed to win it all, Allen Iverson's sophomore year had been truly impressive. He led the Big East in points and steals per game and was named a First Team All-American as well as the Big East Defensive Player of the Year for the second straight year.

Georgetown basketball players under Coach Thompson were expected to stay for four years, and Iverson seriously considered returning for his junior year. However, Iverson could not just think about himself. As the man of the Iverson family, he had to take care of his mother as well as his two younger sisters. Iverson believed that the best way to do so would be to secure an NBA contract as soon as possible. Thus, he declared for the NBA Draft. Coach Thompson hated to see Iverson leave but he respected his guard's decision and claimed that he was the best guard in Georgetown basketball history. Seventeen years later, he would be present for Allen Iverson's retirement ceremony in Philadelphia.

Chapter 4: Allen's Early Years in the NBA

Getting Drafted

The 1996 NBA Draft Class goes down in history as one of the best batches of young rookies the league has ever seen. When it came down to it, the class of 1996 had a whopping total of 58 All-Star appearances when all of the members had retired. This draft class also produced 14 NBA championships and is widely considered the best as far as star talent and accomplishments are concerned. Of course, the class' headliner remained to be Allen Iverson, who turned heads and wowed everyone with his amazing performances in Georgetown.

Listed initially as a point guard because of his size, Allen Iverson was measured to be a lean 6'1" player. However, some may even think 6'1" is already generous for Iverson. He was barely 6 feet tall. With that lack of size, Allen Iverson was obviously a small player even for a point guard. He made up for his small stature with his heart and his exceptional offensive capabilities and physical attributes.

When it came down to it, nobody in the draft class could keep up with Allen Iverson as far as athleticism was concerned. He was lighting quick. He was blazing fast. He could run circles around the defense all game long without showing any bit of fatigue. On top of his legendary speed and quickness, Allen Iverson had a lot of hops in his slight and tiny stature. He was a physical specimen trapped in the body of a 6 foot tall college sophomore.

Coming into the draft, Allen Iverson was often compared to legendary Detroit Pistons player Isiah Thomas. Both players were barely 6 feet tall but played all heart every single game. Like Thomas, Iverson was a great scorer that could also make plays for others. He was not considered a true point guard, but had the skills to be on par with the likes of Isiah Thomas.

Using his speed and quickness, Allen Iverson's offensive game was predicated on all of his athletic abilities. He ran the floor effortlessly. No defender could keep up with him whether he had the ball in his hands or not. That was why Allen Iverson scored the bulk of his points. He used his blinding foot speed to race past defenders and get to the basket. He made fast break opportunities possible even if there were not any. He was that fast. He made transition opportunities look effortless.

On the half court set, Allen Iverson has a fantastic set of dribbling maneuvers that he pairs up with his quickness to easily get to the basket. He often utilizes an adept array of dribbles and crossover moves that keep heads spinning and turning. He breaks ankles with ease on his way to the basket. As far as incoming rookies were concerned, Iverson's ball handles were already at an elite level compared to even all the other NBA veterans.

With all of his athletic gifts and skills at getting to the basket, what made Allen Iverson a unique offensive talent were his finishing abilities at the basket. He makes converting baskets inside the shaded area look so easy despite his meager size. Allen Iverson absorbs the contact, contorts his body, and lays the ball up high to avoid the shot blockers and finishes strong at the rim. His heart at finishing plays at the basket all but makes up for his lack of size.

On the defensive end, Allen Iverson is also an excellent asset for any team. Despite his size, he uses his athletic abilities to keep up with his defenders. His heart and competitive edge help him fight against the bigger offensive players. And nobody in the draft class was better than him at getting steals up front or in the passing lanes. His hands were always just as quick as his feet when it came down to pilfering possessions from opposing offensive players.

Despite his incredible athletic gifts, his polished offensive game, and his penchant for playing the defensive end of the floor exceptionally well, Allen Iverson did have some chinks and weaknesses in his armor despite being the best prospect in the 1996 NBA Draft. The first of Iverson's weaknesses was, of course, his lack of size and height.

Even at the point guard position, Allen Iverson's generous 6'0" frame was often regarded as a weakness. His size was a cause for concern especially at the NBA level where players knew how to exploit their defender's lack of height and weak frame. And when it came to the paint defenders, the NBA is full of elite shot blockers that were at levels above the ones that Allen Iverson used to score over in college. Size is always a premium in the NBA. Allen Iverson severely lacked that part of the game.

On the offensive end, Allen Iverson may be a polished and complete scorer when it came down to breaking down defenses at the perimeter and scoring well in the paint. However, Iverson did not have a refined jump shot. He was so used to breaking ankles and turning heads out on the perimeter before finishing strong at the basket that he almost never relied on his jump shot. He did show flashes of brilliance with his perimeter shooting, but it remained inconsistent at best. It was a part of his offensive game that needed a lot of work especially when defenders take away his penetration at the NBA level.

On the mental side of the game, Allen Iverson gets so into his scoring world that he often gets erratic and out-of-control. He always had a lot of confidence in his game and often forgot he had teammates. Iverson always had a shoot-first mentality to the detriment of the other players on the court. This was the main reason why he might never be a full-time point guard in the NBA. Point guards often made it a point to make their teammates look better. However, Allen Iverson focused more on getting his own shot rather than getting his teammates going. Such confidence in his ability to dominate the game despite the odds telling him not to was a turn off in a league that puts a lot of premium on guards that shared the ball.

But even with his weaknesses, there was no denying that Allen Iverson was the best prospect of that legendary and historic 1996 Draft Class. And that was saying a lot considering all the other talents available that year. There was defensive juggernaut Marcus Camby at center. Forwards like Shareef Abdur-Rahim and Antoine Walker were also exceptional picks. But the guard spot was the deepest. Along with Iverson, Stephon Marbury and Ray Allen were also considered top prospects. Then there were mysterious but potentially talented youngsters like the 17-year-old Kobe Bryant, who dominated the high school ranks, and underrated point guard Steve Nash from Canada.

But compared to all of those other talented athletes, Allen Iverson stood out because of his heart and polished offensive game. He would be chosen by the Philadelphia 76ers with the top overall draft choice of the 1996 NBA Draft because he was the readiest out of the crop to contribute immediately to a struggling franchise looking to inject itself with star talent. While Marbury, Allen, Bryant, and Nash all ended up becoming legendary players, they did not have Allen Iverson's immediate impact and star prowess at the get-go.

The 1997 Rookie of the Year

In 1996, the Philadelphia 76ers desperately needed a boost. Ever since trading Hall of Fame power forward, Charles Barkley, in 1992, they had not won more than 26 games in each of the next four seasons. In fact, they only won 18 games in the season before they drafted Iverson. Even though they had received high draft picks due to their miserable record, they failed to convert them into useful players. They selected Shawn Bradley in 1993 and Sharone Wright in 1994. But with Iverson, the 76ers had their best chance yet at moving past the Barkley era and reinvigorating the Philadelphia fan base. 76ers management hoped that Iverson and future All-Star shooting guard, Jerry Stackhouse, would form a terrific offensive duo.

In Iverson's first NBA game on November 1, 1996, he showed some of that early promise by converting 12 out of 19 field goals including three out of four behind the three-point line to finish with 30 points in a 111-103 loss to the Milwaukee Bucks. After only 15 points and 24 points against the Chicago Bulls and Detroit Pistons in the next two games, Iverson would score 32 points after making 9 out of 19 field goals. He also had 14 out of 22 free throws to help Philadelphia get their first win of the season against the Boston Celtics, 115-105, on November 8, 1996. He had a mix of good games and bad games including only six points after shooting 3 out of 10 from the field in a 112-95 win over the Phoenix Suns on November 9, 1996. Iverson would collect eight assists for his teammates for offensive scoring opportunities.

While Iverson was still young in the NBA, he was improving on offense throughout the season. He nearly had his first triple-double in a 109-92 win over the New York Knicks on November 23, 1996. Iverson scored 26 points while collecting nine rebounds and nine assists. In the next game, Iverson would get his first career double-double with 16 points and ten rebounds on November 26, 1996, in a 100-88 loss to the Los

Angeles Lakers. He would get another one in the next game on November 29, 1996, in a 100-91 win over the Orlando Magic where Iverson finished with 14 points and ten rebounds. It was a good first month, but he would have a better second month despite the losses for Philadelphia.

On December 5, 1996, Iverson scored 36 points and had 11 assists during a 106-102 loss in Dallas, which was followed with 35 points and seven rebounds in a losing effort at Houston on December 7, 1996, 123-108. He would have some games where he would score 30 or more points, but then there were also nights where he would make anywhere between 15 to 20 points on nights where he would struggle from the field. His trips to the foul line, however, offsets the final statistical line.

For example, Iverson had 37 points in a 111-107 loss to the Indiana Pacers on January 19, 1997, despite only converting 9 out of 24 field goals but he made 17 of 19 free throws. One of his worst games concerning field goal percentage was on January 24, 1997, where he would make only 5 of 17 (29.4%) with six free throws in to finish with 16 points. There were more offensive struggles in the month of February 1997, where the most points Iverson scored was 25 against the San Antonio Spurs on February 5, 1997, in a 113-97 win. Beyond that, there were several games where he scored less than 15 points, including a rough game on February 26, 1997, making only eight points after making 3 out of 15 field goals in a 111-104 loss. During that month, Iverson only averaged 16.4 points per game while making only 32.7% from the field. Those numbers would improve in March with an average of 22.6 points per game and an improved 46.2% during that 14-game span.

With those kinds of performances from the shifty and surprising newcomer, there was no doubt who the top rookie was that season. He was described as erratic, especially with the way he played. He would have a great scoring and shooting night one day before going blank from the field in his next game. He was mercurial. There were no middle parts for Allen Iverson in his rookie year. He was all extremes. Either he was making all of his shots or was shooting bricks. But the only thing that remained consistent was his sky-high confidence.

As Iverson would say, one bad game did not make him lose his confidence. He still had all the confidence in the world to force himself into dominating one game after an awful one. But even with his supreme confidence, he knew that he still had a lot left to prove. He would not admit that he was having a good season. In fact, he knew for a fact that he will get better. Allen Iverson was a confident man that remained humble in his game knowing that there were still others better than him. A bad game did not deter him. Good ones only made him more confident.

A case in point was when Allen Iverson had one game with 37 points against the Chicago Bulls on March 12, 1996. Despite the 108-104 loss, Iverson showed his skills against one of the best by beating Michael Jordan with a terrific crossover – not bad for a rookie. It was one of his biggest moments as an NBA player. That move was Iverson's defining moment as an NBA star. Michael Jordan was a former Defensive Player of the Year. Even at his advanced age, he was still the best two-way player in the league. He may not have been the quickest player at that point, but he was still an intelligent defender. But Allen Iverson made it look like he owned the Greatest Player of All Time. At least for one play.

The best player in the world was defending the best rookie on that one play. Allen Iverson, with all his self-confidence, was not afraid of the five-time MVP and, at that time, the four-time NBA champion. He sized up His Airness by pulling off one of his patented quick crossovers from the left to right to see if the legendary player would bite while the Philadelphia crowd was cheering on to what they were witnessing. Michael Jordan bit hard thinking AI was going to the left. That gave Iverson enough room to pull off the legendary jump shot that made him an instant icon.

Despite that legendary performance against arguably the greatest to ever play the game, Allen Iverson's best games were in the last month of the season where he averaged 33.6 points and 8.7 assists in April. Iverson would reach the 40-point mark for the first time on April 5, 1997, in a 115-113 loss to the Charlotte Hornets with 44 points from making 12 out of 18 field goals, two out of three from beyond the three-point arc, and six for seven from the foul line. It was also an excellent overall individual performance with ten rebounds, seven assists, and three steals.

But it would not be the last game where he had at least 40 points. In fact, Iverson had five straight games where he scored 40 points or more, breaking the NBA record set by Wilt Chamberlain in 1959. Iverson would score 40 points against the Atlanta Hawks on April 9, 1997, followed by another 44 points on April 11 against the Milwaukee Bucks. The best game of this five-game scorings streak was on April 12 in Cleveland where Iverson converted 17 of 32 field goals (43.1%), which included making five out of nine three-pointers (55.6%) and making 11 out of 18 free throws to end the night with his first 50-point game.

The streak ended with another 40 points on April 14, 1997, against the Washington Bullets (before the name-change to the Wizards). While it was an impressive run, the 76ers did not win any of those games. In fact, they would only win on April 16, 1997, against the New Jersey Nets, 113-105, while Iverson only scored 27 points with 11 assists.

Philadelphia would finish with a record of 22-60, which was good for second to last place in the Atlantic Division and was barely better than the worst team in the Eastern Conference (Boston, 15-67). The team performance may not have been a lot better from the previous season, but the emergence and injection of Allen Iverson into the system gave hope to what was then considered a dying franchise. Iverson gave the city of Philadelphia a superstar they could cheer and rely on to usher a new era of basketball consistency.

Despite the poor record, Iverson would be named the NBA's Rookie of the Year for 1997, and that is because he averaged 23.5 points thanks to a 41.6 field goal percentage and making about 34.1 percent of all shot attempts beyond the three-point arc. Iverson also averaged 7.5 assists, 4.1 rebounds, and 2.1 steals in that first season in Philadelphia. While he was not selected to participate in the NBA's All-Star Game, Iverson was part of the overall weekend when he participated in the 1997

NBA Rising Stars game on February 8, 1997, that featured each conference and their best rookies and second-season players. Iverson helped the East defeat the West, 96-91, with 19 points, nine assists, and four rebounds to become the game's most valuable player.

It was a great season for an improving young Allen Iverson, who brought a lot of flair and excitement in the era when the NBA was seeking its next great star. He had a penchant for doing the most spectacular thing he could do, whether it was in his dribbling or passing. Iverson was an instant fan favorite because of the heart and passion he showed for the game even as a rookie.

However, it was not all without criticism. Allen Iverson, for all his youth and relative inexperience, was thrust into a superstar role that, despite his confidence, he was not yet ready to handle. It was all obvious from his stats. He was averaging 40 minutes per game and was among the league's top five in shot attempts. And despite the number of shots he was taking, Allen Iverson was shooting a poor clip from the field compared to all the other players shooting more or the same amount of shots he was taking. His turnovers were also tops in the league. He was still too inexperienced and immature to know when to stick to a basic play or when to go for the spectacular. This caused him to lose possessions in bunches.

But despite that, Allen Iverson's Rookie of the Year campaign gave hope to a city that needed a lot of it. It gave the NBA the hope it needed as it was becoming clear that Michael Jordan was on his last legs as an NBA player. He was going to be the bridge from the 90's era that had attitude and talent to the 2000's era where young and fresh legs were soaring high in the NBA. He was the front man of that legendary 1996 NBA Draft Class.

The Sophomore Slump

In the 1997-1998 season, the 76ers hired Coach Larry Brown. Brown had previously coached the Indiana Pacers to multiple appearances in the Eastern Conference Finals, but he now wanted to coach the 76ers because Iverson's talent intrigued him. However, Brown was a coach famous for wanting to play "the right way," and he was determined to mold Iverson into a traditional point guard who sought to pass first and score second. Iverson and Brown would repeatedly clash over their different visions for the next several years. However, there was no other coach Iverson respected more than Larry Brown.

The 76ers management tinkered with how to build the team around Iverson. Jerry Stackhouse was traded for a defensive center, Theo Ratliff. Other defensive players, like point guards Eric Snow and Aaron McKie, were brought in as well. Philadelphia's offense efficiency as measured by offensive rating ranked 21st both in the 1996-1997 and 1997-1998 seasons, but their defense as measured by defensive rating improved from 26th to 18th. The result was that the 76ers improved, winning 31 games in Larry Brown's first season as head coach.

But if Philadelphia had developed because of their defense, Iverson was the heart and soul of their offense. Brown tried to have Iverson dominate the ball less, and the result was satisfactory for the time being. While Iverson's scoring decreased from 23.5 to 22 points per game, his field percentage improved to 46 percent, the highest of his career. Iverson's assist-to-turnover ratio also significantly improved, which showed that he could pass the ball as well if he seriously thought about it.

The early signs that clearly showed how Larry Brown wanted his prized young star to play the point guard role often was displayed by the fact that AI had two early games of dishing out double-digit assists. He had 11 assists on top of the 21 points he scored in a five-point loss to the Atlanta Hawks in his second game of the season. Then, on November 9, he would have 23 points and ten dimes in another loss. This time it was against legendary defensive point guard Gary Payton and the Seattle SuperSonics (now Oklahoma City Thunder).

On November 12, 1997, Iverson had a season best of 15 assists during a 114-100 win. Iverson would still lead the team with 26 points to lead all Philadelphia players after making 11 out of 17 field goals (64.7%). The newly acquired Jerry Stackhouse brought instant benefits with 17 points in that game. With that pass first mentality, Iverson had 11 of his 12 double-doubles with double-figure assists. He had either eight or nine assists in another 11 games. Rebounding, however, was not a strong point for a player who was only six-feet tall and about 165 pounds. Iverson had 12 assists in a loss to the Orlando Magic on November 22, 1997, and in a win over the New Jersey Nets on February 21, 1998.

There were a lot less games where Iverson would score 40 or more points, with the lone game hitting that mark on April 10, 1998 in a 107-102 loss to the Minnesota Timberwolves. Iverson had 43 points after converting 15 out of 26 field goals (57.7%), 12 out of 14 foul shots, four rebounds, two assists, and one steal for good measure. However, Iverson was still scoring 30 or more points in about 15 of the games in his second NBA season. He also had one of his best games, statistically, on March 13, 1998, in a 107-86 win over the Atlanta Hawks where he scored

34 points after shooting 15 out of 26 from the field while also having ten assists and six rebounds.

On March 18, 1998, Iverson made 12 of 22 field goals (54.5%) and 14 out of 16 free throws (87.5%) to score 38 points in the team's 104-96 win over the Detroit Pistons, on the road. In Brown's first season as the head coach in Philadelphia, the 76ers finished the season with a record of 31-51 as the last-place team in the Atlantic Division, but they were far from the worst team, which was the Toronto Raptors with a record of 16-66. Iverson would finish the season averaging 22 points per game, as well as 6.2 assists, and held a 46.1 field goal percentage.

But even with the steady game he had as a sophomore player, Allen Iverson still saw a slump that had forced him to tone down his statistics. He was still adjusting to the new system that Brown wanted him to play. Moreover, Allen Iverson was playing the role of the point guard more traditionally. He decreased his shot attempts while shooting a personal career best 46.1% from the floor.

Allen Iverson also was not selected as an All-Star even though he was playing better than all of his 1996 NBA draftmates. Instead, a fellow 1996 draftee was even chosen to be an All-Star ahead of him. It was the then 19-year-old Kobe Bryant who, though was not putting up the numbers that AI did, was showing early signs of becoming the next Michael Jordan. It also helped Bryant that he was playing for a popular team like the Los Angeles Lakers.

Allen Iverson's mini struggles in his sophomore season also proved something else. It was clear that he was not a traditional point guard. No amount of coaching or training would ever change his identity as a scorer. That was what made Allen Iverson special. Despite early comparisons, he was not an Isiah Thomas player that wanted to both score and facilitate. He was out there on the floor to put points up on the board. He was a scorer, not a facilitator.

The Rise of Allen Iverson, His First Scoring Title

In the 1998-1999 season, Larry Brown made a bold move in the starting lineup. Iverson had been the starting point guard in his first two seasons, and Brown made Eric Snow the new point guard while Iverson would be the starting shooting guard. Initially, such a move seemed insane. How was the less than six-foot Iverson going to guard bigger guards like Reggie Miller or Penny Hardaway?

The answer was that on defense, Snow would guard the opposing shooting guard while Iverson would guard the point guard. Meanwhile, on offense, the opponent's shooting guard would guard Iverson. The shooting guard's size would work against him then, as he would lack the agility needed to keep up with Iverson. But then again, there was also a profound lack of good shooting guards back then. Allen Iverson pounced on that.

The starting lineup change worked. As the shooting guard, Iverson now had more freedom under Brown's system to score. The 1998-1999 season lasted 50 frenetic games due to a lockout which favored athletic players who could handle the tougher, more compressed schedule like Iverson. However, it took some time for Iverson to find his scoring groove. In the first three games, Iverson averaged 16.7 points per game in three wins over the Charlotte Hornets, Orlando Magic, and Detroit Pistons. However, he had a field goal percentage of 27.3 and 21.4% from behind the three-point line.

They would suffer their first loss of the season on February 12, 1999, at home against the San Antonio Spurs where he scored 46 points after converting only 14 out of 26 from the field (53.8%) and made 15 out of 17 free throws. After that, he was keeping his point totals each game above 20 points and often entered the 30-point range with a few 40-point appearances like the one mentioned above.

One of his better performances after that 46-point outburst was when he had 37 points, seven rebounds, and nine assists while shooting 12 out of 22 from the field in a win over the Cleveland Cavaliers on February 22. It was a game that launched a six-game winning streak for the Philadelphia 76ers. In that winning streak, AI had four games of scoring above 30 points. His lowest output during that run was only 25 points.

On March 19, 1999, Iverson scored 41 points and ten assists in Philadelphia's 105-90 win over the Los Angeles Lakers. This was two days after Iverson scored 39 points on 13 of 21 (61.9%) shooting overall. He also had seven rebounds, three assists, two steals, and one block in that game. He had a hand in all parts of the game between offense and defense.

Allen Iverson would not hold on to that torrid scoring pace and would see a minor slump of inconsistent performances during the early parts of April. Nevertheless, he was still able to put up a high of 38 points during that month. He made 15 out of 28 field goals in that April 25, 1999, win against the Orlando Magic. He also added seven assists and four steals to his tally.

As the dust settled, Iverson's field goal percentage dropped to 41%, but he compensated for that by driving past slower shooting guards and drawing free throws. Iverson averaged 26.8 points per game and grabbed his first NBA scoring title. The post-Michael Jordan era served him well as no other guard or player in the league could put up points in bunches as well as he did. Shaquille O'Neal closely trailed him for that accolade, but it was already clear who the best scorer in the league was.

Allen Iverson also had 4.6 assists per game and even grabbed 4.9 rebounds despite his diminutive status. There was no All-Star game due to the shortened season, but Iverson was nominated to the All-NBA First Team. Had there been an All-Star Game, he would have surely been a starter particularly since fans and voters were still recovering from Jordan's second retirement. Most importantly, the 76ers had a 28-22 record and finally made the NBA playoffs for the first time since 1991. Their defense improved from 18th to 5th.

The 76ers faced off against the Orlando Magic in the first round of the 1999 NBA playoffs. Orlando had home-court advantage for the series and was led by their star shooting guard, Penny Hardaway. In the duel between the two star guards, Iverson came out on top. In his playoff debut, he scored 30 points to Hardaway's 19 as Philadelphia struck first with the 104-90

Game 1 win on May 9, 1999. Hardaway and the Magic would win a defensive battle in the second game of the series on May 11, 1999, where Orlando would take the 79-68 decision. Iverson struggled, shooting only 4 out of 15 (26.7%) for 13 points. However, the 76ers would bounce back to close out the best-of-five series.

In Game 3 on May 13, 1999, in Philadelphia, Iverson set an NBA playoff record with ten steals in addition to 33 points during a 97-85 win. Most double-doubles usually happen when players get 10 or more rebounds or, in a guard like Iverson's case, assists. It was also a game where Iverson was able to rebound offensively with 14 out of 28 field goals made and about three out of eight from behind the three-point line.

On May 15, 1999, the 76ers were able to complete the upset of the Magic after defeating Orlando 101-91 where Iverson made 14 out of 27 field goals, including four of six three-point attempts, for a field goal percentage of 51.9 and 37 points. Iverson also finished the game with nine assists and two steals. During the 3-1 series win, Iverson averaged 28 points for the series on 44% shooting, while Hardaway had just 19 points on 31 percent.

The Indiana Pacers swept Philadelphia in the next round with Iverson scoring 28.8 points per game while only converting about 38.3% of his field goals – including a 35-point performance in the Game 1 loss in Indianapolis, Indiana on May 17, 1999, and a 32 points in Game 3 on May 21, 1999. Despite the disappointing end to the season, Iverson hoped to build on his strong playoff debut.

Chapter 5: Rising All-Star

Embracing the Superstar Status

The rise of Allen Iverson as one of the premier young stars in a league looking for the next big name to usher in a new era prompted the Philadelphia 76ers management to keep their superstar on a long-term basis. Iverson would sign a $70 million contract extension to stay with the Philadelphia 76ers for the next six years. It was a deal that showed how much the franchise trusted their future to their brash and erratic young star.

The 1999-2000 season showed that the 76ers were truly an up-and-coming team. Philadelphia management continued to shuffle players around Iverson in the hope of building a proper team around him. It was a team that focused more on the defensive end of the game rather than the offense. The role players were built to play defense. Meanwhile, the offensive end of the floor was solely meant for Allen Iverson alone. He had free range to do whatever he wanted to do on offense.

Iverson's three-point shooting also improved to 34% per game, and his scoring took another leap to 28 points per game. A good example of this improved long-distance shot was seen early in the season on November 11, 1999. Iverson was five for six from behind the three-point arc as part of an overall 18 for 33 field goal (54.5%) shooting night where he finished with 46 points in a 110-105 loss to the Orlando Magic.

A few days later, Iverson made four out of five three-pointers as part of a 12 for 25 field goal performance for 30 points in Philadelphia's 93-90 win in Toronto on November 14, 1999. He also made five for six for three points during a 95-73 win on November 16, 1999, a game where Iverson made 13 out of 27 total field goals for 39 points while collecting five rebounds, five assists, and five steals.

Three-point shooting was not the only realm where Allen Iverson stayed consistent. His overall offensive game was as consistent as any could get. One case in point was on December 23, 1999, when he had 42 points on an 11 out of 26 shooting night from the field and 17 out of 20 from the free throw line. It came in a loss to the New Jersey Nets.

On January 3, 2000, Allen Iverson would welcome a new millennium by dropping another game of scoring at least 40 points. In that win against the Milwaukee Bucks, he would go for 45 points on 16 out of 38 shooting from the field and 11 out of 18 shooting from the foul line. Not slowing himself down in the year 2000, AI would go for 34 points just two nights later in a win against the Golden State Warriors.

The next time Allen Iverson would go for at least 40 points was on February 3, 2000, in a loss to the Houston Rockets. He made 16 of his 25 field goal attempts that game. It was a rare sighting for him to be shooting above 60% while scoring an immensely high amount of points. But the best was yet to come for Allen Iverson.

Exactly one game later, AI would go for a new career high of 50 points in a win against the Sacramento Kings. He made 50% of his 40 shots in that game while also grabbing nine rebounds and dishing out six assists in the process. Out of those 50 points Iverson scored, only one field goal was behind the three-point arc. Many of his baskets were from driving towards the basket and making plenty of short to mid-range jump shots. Not to outdo himself, he would go for 41 points just three days after that 50-point outburst in was in a win over the New Jersey Nets.

That was not the only work Iverson had during the NBA's All-Star weekend. He was part of the NBA's Three-Point Shootout competition as one of eight players. It was not his best scoring opportunity, and he had just 10 points in that first round to finish just above Cleveland's Bob Sura in last place. The competition was won by Utah's Jeff Hornacek, who scored 13 in the final round to defeat Dallas' Dirk Nowitzki and Milwaukee's Ray Allen.

As the first half of the season progressed, Iverson scored more, and part of that is due to the increased number of field goal attempts he would take per game. By the end of the season, he averaged nearly 25 field goals per game, and while he would have games where he kept the ball to himself, he maintained a decent percentage by making 42.1% from the field and about 34.1% beyond the three-point line.

Because of Iverson becoming more of an offensive-focused player and keeping the ball more on scoring opportunities, he only had one double-double on March 19, 2000, in a game where he scored 18 points and had ten assists during an 89-85 win over the Orlando Magic. He almost had a triple-double with nine steals in the match, showing that Iverson was still an excellent defensive player in addition to his scoring abilities. He has been close only a few more times with nine rebounds against the Seattle SuperSonics (November 8, 1999) and the Sacramento Kings (February 6, 2000). Likewise, he had nine assists against the Utah Jazz (March 17, 2000).

In 2000, Iverson was nominated to his first All-Star Game held on February 13, 2000, at the Oakland Arena in Oakland, California. In fact, Iverson had nearly two million votes to become one of the five starters for the Eastern Conference and had the third most of all players behind Vince Carter of the Toronto Raptors (1,911,973 votes) and Alonzo Mourning of the Miami Heat (1,878,588 votes).

Iverson did not disappoint the fans who supported him as he finished with 26 points in 28 minutes after making 10 out of 18 field goals, which includes both of his two attempts for three-pointers. He also finished with nine assists, a couple of rebounds, and one steal on defense. However, the West would get the win, 137-126. Minnesota's Kevin Garnett and San Antonio's Tim Duncan had 24 points, and Shaquille O'Neal scored 22 of his own.

It was after the All-Star Game when Allen Iverson led a fierce nine-game winning streak to help his team secure a good spot in the playoffs. During that winning streak, Iverson broke the 40-point barrier twice. He had 44 on March 22, 2000 against the Toronto Raptors. Six days after that, he would go for 43 points on 15 out of 28 shooting from the field against the Minnesota Timberwolves.

The 76ers won 49 games to finish third in the Atlantic Division and fifth in the Eastern Conference behind their stout team defense and Iverson's offense. They once again qualified for the playoffs and defeated the Charlotte Hornets in the first round. Once again, Iverson was the leader of the team by using his offensive abilities which were showcased in the first game that Philadelphia won 92-82 on April 22, 2000. He was 13 of 25 from the field (52%) and converted all three of his three-point attempts. He also made 11 of 16 free throws to go along with five rebounds, three assists, and three steals.

However, when Iverson struggled, so did the team. After all, he was the main reason why the Philadelphia 76ers were even putting points up on the board in the first place. Allen Iverson was not the Sixers' primary offensive weapon, but rather their only source of offense. In the second game on April 24, 2000, Charlotte won 108-98 as Iverson made only five out of 21 total field goals to score only 13 points as lesser known star Toni Kukoc led the 76ers with 20 points off the bench followed by Eric Snow's 19 points and Theo Ratliff's 19 points.

But the defense was still stout during the series, and the 76ers even held the Hornets to less than 80 points in the third game on April 28, 2000, as Philadelphia won 81-76. The 76ers would finish out the series on May 1, 2000, with a 105-99 win to clinch the best-of-five series, 3-1. Iverson was able to score 26 points to go along with seven assists, and his two teammates had double-doubles to provide support for the win. Aaron McKie had 25 points and 11 assists while Matt Geiger had 17 points and ten rebounds off the bench.

But once again, Philadelphia found themselves facing the Indiana Pacers in the second round of the NBA playoffs. Iverson remained strong offensively despite the Pacers taking the first three games of the best of seven series, including 28 points and ten assists for a double-double in a 103-97 loss on May 8, 2000. In Game 2, Iverson was missing many field goals and only made 9 out of 25. He made 9 out of 21 from the field for a team-leading 29 points in the Game 3 loss, 97-89, on May 10, 2000. In the playoff series during the previous season, the 76ers were swept by the Pacers, and there were concerns that this would be the same fate.

Everyone expected the Philadelphia 76ers to lose the entire series. After all, no team in league history has ever come back from a 0-3 deficit to win it all. Some teams have tried, but would ultimately fail. The fate of the Sixers was all but sealed. The only question was whether they would quickly succumb to it or if they would go down fighting. Judging from Allen

Iverson's heart for the game, it was clear that he was not going to fold so easily to the superior team.

Philadelphia started to find a team mojo in Game 4 on May 13, 2000, in a 92-90 win. Iverson led the team with 19 points despite only shooting 26.9 percent from the field, which made it necessary for his teammates to step up, including Tyrone Hill's 19 points and 15 rebounds. The 76ers would also have five players score into double digits led by Iverson's 37 points in a 107-86 win on May 15, 2000. Ratliff had 26 points and nine rebounds. Other teammates gave their contribution, like McKie (13 points, ten rebounds), and Hill (12 points, ten rebounds) who each had double-doubles as the team converted 50 percent of their total field goals.

However, the 76ers were not able to maintain that to tie the series in Philadelphia on May 19, 2000, in a 106-90 loss to Indiana for the 4-2 series conclusion. Iverson was seven for 20 from the field for 18 points as the team finished with 39.1% from the field. Iverson was thoroughly outplayed by Indiana star shooting guard, Reggie Miller. Iverson took almost twice as many shots per game as Miller but barely managed to outscore him per game.

After the season ended, head coach, Larry Brown, was furious with Iverson for what he felt to be his star guard's continued inability to pass the ball. During the 2000 offseason, Philadelphia seriously considered trading Iverson and began negotiations for a four-team deal with Detroit, the Los Angeles Lakers, and Charlotte. Fortunately for Philadelphia, the trade negotiations fell through. It was extremely difficult to trade a 24-year-old shooting forward who averaged 28.4 points per game. It turned out that he was about to have even better seasons coming up.

The MVP Season

The 2000-2001 season would be the best of Iverson's career. He ultimately took over the offense and became a lethal threat on the court. He was still at his best crossing over opponents and taking it the ball to the rack against bigger defenders. But now he had a legitimate jump shot and drew more free throws than ever before.

The improved Philadelphia 76ers and a much more mature Allen Iverson would lead his team to the best start the franchise has ever had. The Philadelphia 76ers would open the season with ten consecutive wins. Oddly enough, Allen Iverson did not even put up terrific scoring numbers during that run. He would only score a high of 29 points in that historic opening for the franchise.

As the season went on, the winning numbers began to normalize for the Philadelphia 76ers while Allen Iverson proceeded to score in bunches as he usually did. He would go for a then-season high of 45 points on 15 out of 34 shooting in a loss to the Utah Jazz on December 20. The game before that, he had 33 points in a win over the Chicago Bulls.

On January 6, 2001, Iverson scored a career-high 54 points against the Cleveland Cavaliers in a 107-103 win on the road where he would convert 20 out of 30 field goals with 4 out of 7 from the three-point range and 10 out of 13 free throws in what was a career high at the time. Amazingly, he did not tire out after going for 41 points in a big 32-point win against the Seattle SuperSonics just the game before that career output.

It would not take long for AI to go for at least 40 points again. On January 13, 2001, he had 40 in a win against the San Antonio Spurs despite the latter's tough defensive strategies. Four days later, he had 43 in a win against the Chicago Bulls. About two weeks after his career 54-point game, on January 21, 2001, he scored 51 points against the Toronto Raptors. Even though the 76ers lost 110-106 that night, Iverson was the star as he made 20 out of 40 field goals – four of eight in three-point field goal attempts – and also had four assists, three rebounds, and one steal.

In addition to those 50-point games, Iverson was still often shooting with an average of about 25-and-a- half field goals per game and converting about 42% of his total shots. That allowed Iverson to have 15 additional games where he scored 40 or more points, many of which were during games where he attempted at least 30 field goals.

Among those high 40-point outputs were the three consecutive ones he had in the middle of February right before the All-Star break. He started off with 49 points on 17 out of 32 shooting against the Milwaukee Bucks. He proceeded to score 40 points on 14 out of 29 shooting from the field versus the LA Lakers after that. He then rounded up the fervent scoring performances by going for 42 points against the Clippers this time. All three games were wins.

On February 23, 2001, Allen Iverson put to rest questions about his ability to play both the role of a facilitator and a scorer. In that huge 21-point win against the Detroit Pistons, Iverson poured 43 big points on another good defensive team. On top of that, he got his teammates going by dishing out ten dimes in the process. It was a rare 40-point double-double game for a guard considering that players like Allen Iverson only had two options on offense—to pass or to shoot. Allen Iverson would have four more games of scoring at least 40 points as the season neared its end.

Philadelphia made a huge leap when they traded for Dikembe Mutombo in February. The 7'2" center was never the greatest offensive force, but he was a defensive monster. Iverson and Mutombo combined to form an incredible tandem, and the Philadelphia 76ers finished with a record of 56-26 to take the top spot in the Atlantic Division for the first time in several years. It was also a rare moment for the team to have the top seed in the Eastern Conference and to be one of the favorites that could win the NBA Championship that season.

For his individual efforts, Iverson was nominated to the All-Star Team and the All-NBA First Team once again, but his biggest achievement was earning the Most Valuable Player Award. Mutombo, on the other hand, was awarded the Defensive Player of the Year. Allen Iverson's MVP award was not even a question. He won 93 first place votes out of a total of 124. The nearest to him was Tim Duncan, who only had 18 first place votes.

The award solidified Allen Iverson's place as one of the most elite players in the entire league. He did not have the size, but he was all heart every single night for a team that did not seem like it would belong amongst the top contenders in the league. While the Sixers had good role players, nobody else was near the All-Star production of AI. The nearest was Theo Ratliff, who was putting up 12.4 points per game. The rest, like Dikembe Mutombo, were all defensive specialist. Simply put, Allen Iverson was the entire Philadelphia 76ers' offense. He was their heart and soul.

For the season, Iverson scored 31.1 points per game along with 4.6 assists and 3.8 rebounds. Iverson also impressed viewers, not just with his scoring, but also with his defense. He compensated for his size with the heart and toughness and could strip the ball away from anyone who was not taking care of it. He averaged 2.5 steals per game and had six games where he had five or more steals. Up to that point in his career, Iverson had been one of the best guards in the league. He had already become the best little man in the history of the NBA.

But it was the 2001 NBA Playoffs that would secure his legacy. In the first round, Philadelphia got their revenge against the Indiana Pacers who had knocked them out twice before. The first game of the series had some fans worrying that recent history would repeat itself as the Pacers won a defensive battle, 79-78, on April 21, 2001. The 76ers was cold, shooting only39.7%. Iverson salvaged 16 points while only making 7 out of 19 field goals. That cold shooting would not last long, however, as Philadelphia bounced back in Game 2 with a 116-98 victory on April 24, 2001as Iverson converted 15 out of 27 field goals (55.6%) to finish with 45 points, nine assists, and a couple of steals thrown in. Iverson's shooting also included three for seven from deep range and making 12 out of 14 free throws to help him lead everyone in scoring, beating out Indiana's Reggie Miller, who scored 41 points from 14 of 22 from the field (63.6%).

Iverson followed that up with 32 points, seven rebounds, and six assists in all but one minute of action on the court as Philadelphia defeated Indiana in Game 3, 92-87, on April 28, 2001. The series was clinched on May 2, 2001, as they would win 88-85 with Iverson leading the team with 33 points despite making only 10 out of his 31 field goal attempts. At the time, Iverson was going to find a way to get his points regardless of where on the field or the foul line he was going to shoot from. It was also important to note that Mutombo was helping to provide second chances for his team with an average of 14.8

rebounds per game in the four-game series, including 22 collected in Game 1.

Reggie Miller played his heart out and averaged 31 points for the series, but the rest of the Pacers were unable to help him as the 76ers exorcised their demons from Indiana with a 3-1 win in the best-of-five series to open the 2001 playoffs. Iverson finished shooting 41% on the series with averages of 31.5 points, 6.5 assists, and four rebounds per game in all four games.

The second round of the NBA playoffs was an incredible thriller. In 2009, it was nominated by TNT program *Inside the NBA* as one of the best playoff series of the past decade. The 76ers faced off against the Toronto Raptors led by their star shooting guard Vince Carter. While Iverson won fans with his crossover and incredible dribble moves, Carter was the greatest dunker in the league. He had wowed NBA fans with his incredible performance at the 2000 Slam Dunk Contest and famously dunked over a seven-foot Frenchman in the 2000 Olympics.

But Vince Carter was more than just a flashy dunker. He was a great all-around player and was determined to go head-to-head against Iverson. In Game 1, Iverson outscored Carter 36 to 35, but Carter had a crucial tip-in in the final seconds to secure the Toronto win, 96-93, on May 6, 2001. Iverson came right back with a then playoff career-high of 54 points to lead Philadelphia to the 97-97 Game 2 win on May 9, 2001. Iverson made 21 out of 39 field goals (53.8%) along with three of five shots made for three-pointers and a perfect nine for nine from the foul line. Eric Snow was the only other player to score in double digits with 10 points.

Short of telling Iverson "anything you can do, I can do better," Carter responded in Game 3 with 50 points of his own, converting 19 out of 29 from the field and nine out of 13 from three-point range. Toronto would win, 102-78, on May 11, 2001. Iverson had 23 points but was cold as he only made 7 out of his 22 attempts for 31.8 %.

The roles were reversed as Philadelphia took Game 4 on May 13, 2001, as Iverson scored 30 points while Mutombo had 13 points and 17 rebounds to lead the team to an 84-79 win. In the moments before Game 5, on May 16, 2001, at the First Union Center in Philadelphia, there was a special pre-game ceremony held so that the NBA Commissioner David Stern could give Iverson his award as the league's Most Valuable Player. Iverson would hold the trophy above his head to the cheers of the home crowd.

That might have energized the newly crowned MVP to have an individual performance fitting of that title as the 76ers took the 3-2 series lead after winning 121-88. Iverson was 21 of 32 in field goals (65.6 percent), including eight out of 14 behind the three-point arc (57.1 percent), to finish with 52 points, seven assists, and four steals.

The series came down to Game 7. In the final seconds, the 76ers led 88-87, but Vince Carter had the ball for the game and series winner. Fortunately for Iverson, Carter missed, and Philadelphia moved on to the Eastern Conference Finals. McKie was second on the team with 19 points, followed by Mutombo's 14 points. The team finished with 60.3% from the field with 52.4% for all shots in three-point range. The Raptors would bounce back to force a seventh game after their 101-89 win on May 18, 2001, in Toronto, Canada. It was a game when Carter scored 39 points. Iverson, on the other hand, had 20 points after shooting 6 of 24 from the field.

Everything in this series came down to one game where Carter missed a 19-foot shot in the final seconds as the 76ers held off for the 88-87 win on May 20, 2001, giving Philadelphia the 4-3 series win. Iverson did more than just score as he only had 21 points after making 8 out of 27 field goals (29.6%). His 16 assists helped four teammates score in double figures, including

22 points from McKie, and Mutombo having 10 points and 17 rebounds for the double-double.

Philadelphia then faced the Milwaukee Bucks, who were led by Ray Allen, a fellow 1996 draftee who AI had plenty of battles with during college. The series was highly controversial. Iverson shot poorly for most of the series and was outplayed by Allen, who averaged 27 points and shot a ludicrous 51% from three-point range over the series. But Milwaukee lacked any real big men and the 76ers, especially Mutombo, pushed their way into the paint repeatedly and drew fouls. The Bucks complained that the officiating favored the 76ers. While the free throw disparity did support Philadelphia, the difference could be explained by the fact that Milwaukee was more of a jump shooting team.

While Iverson struggled for most of the series, he scored 44 points in the crucial Game 7 on June 3, 2001, in a 108-91 win. Iverson had his best game of the series with 17 of 33 field goals (51.5%), which included four of six behind the three-point line and six of seven free throws. He also had seven assists and six rebounds. It was one of the team's all-around complete games as Mutombo had 23 points and 19 rebounds as one of the team's three double-doubles. McKie had 10 points and 13 assists while

Tyrone Hill had 11 points and ten rebounds. The team shot 45.5% from the field and 50 percent from the three-point range.

As the final seconds ticked away, Allen Iverson headed to the bench. He hugged Larry Brown, the coach who he had fought with so often. Iverson was still able to average 30.5 points per game in that series despite only shooting 34.4% from the field. However, this was a big moment and big test for the 2001 Eastern Conference Champions from Philadelphia. It was one thing to make the NBA Finals. It was another thing to win it by defeating the defending champions, the Los Angeles Lakers.

Philadelphia had won as many regular season games as Los Angeles, but the Lakers and their star center Shaquille O'Neal, in particular, had visibly slacked off during the regular season. They were not slacking off at this point during the playoffs. Los Angeles destroyed their first three opponents in the playoffs, sweeping all of them. In addition to the monstrous numbers that Shaquille O'Neal was putting up, another 1996 draftee was putting up terrific numbers playing alongside the legendary center. Kobe Bryant was also in one of his best playoff forms at that point of the season and was just as valuable as Shaq was for the Lakers.

Given how quickly the Lakers had dispatched the San Antonio Spurs in the Western Conference Finals, no one believed Philadelphia had a chance. Everyone was talking about a potential Lakers playoffs sweep, which would have been the first in NBA history. Of course, nobody in the league could contend with what the Lakers were doing. Shaq and Kobe were dominating the post season. They were two of the best five players in the league at that time. It was a pair of top five players against the top individual performer of the season. However, Allen Iverson was a lonely man on top. He did not have any help with him. All he had was himself. For at least one game, that would be enough.

On basketball's biggest stage, Allen Iverson had the greatest game of his career. In the first half of Game 1 on June 6, 2001, at the Staples Center in Los Angeles, California, Iverson was everywhere. He picked Lakers star shooting guard Kobe Bryant's pocket, hit jump shots, passed the ball, and took the ball to the rim. He scored 30 points by the end of the second quarter. Lakers Coach Phil Jackson sent guard Tyronn Lue to guard Iverson in the second half.

Playing mind games, Lue, who was similar in height and build to Iverson, was dressed similarly to the newly minted MVP. He had the patented cornrow hairstyle that AI made famous. He even wore the arm sleeve that Iverson also patented as one of his best looks. It was like Iverson was looking at a mirror of himself. Lue used his size to prevent Iverson from getting the ball and slowed him down to just 11 points in the second half. At the end of the fourth quarter, both teams were tied at 94.

In the crucial overtime, Iverson took over. He scored seven straight points at the end of overtime. With less than a minute left in the game, Philadelphia led 101-99. Iverson had the basketball with Lue pressuring him. Iverson faked the drive on Lue, then dribbled the ball between his knees and hit the stepback jumper. Lue fell on the ground beside him, and Iverson famously stepped over Lue as he got back on defense. That shot remains to be the most iconic moment in Allen Iverson's career. He had slain a giant team all by his lonesome.

As the stunned Los Angeles crowd watched in disbelief, the 76ers stole Game 1 107-101 and struck the first virtual punch in the mouth. As Iverson walked back into the locker room, he hugged his teammates. "We ain't done nothing yet," he declared. "We've got a long way to go." It was a defining moment for such a young and brave player like Allen Iverson. Nobody even gave them the chance of taking one game away from the defending champions, who swept all the other contenders in the West.

Unfortunately, no truer words were ever spoken. Even with the Defensive Player of the Year, Mutombo, Philadelphia just had no answer for Shaquille O'Neal. O'Neal nearly had a quadruple double (28 points, 20 rebounds, nine assists, and eight blocked shots) in Los Angeles's Game 2 victory on June 8, 2001, 98-89. Philadelphia as a team only made 39.1% of their field goals with Iverson leading the team with 23 points after shooting 34.4% (10 out of 29).

Iverson had a rare double-double during Game 3 back at home on June 10, 2001, with 35 points and 12 rebounds. Mutombo also had a good night with 23 points and 12 rebounds – making nine out of 14 from the field for 64.3%. But the Lakers were led by Kobe Bryant's 32 points, a double-double from O'Neal (30 points, 12 rebounds), and 15 points from Robert Horry coming off the bench. The Lakers took the series lead after winning 96-91. Iverson would score another 35 points after making 12 of 30 field goals and 10 of 14 free throws, but there was not much coming from his teammates on June 13, 2001, as Philadelphia lost 100-86 to fall behind the proverbial eight ball at 3-1 in the series.

During Game 5 on June 15, 2001, in Philadelphia, Iverson had a valiant effort to keep his team in the series after making 14 out of 32 field goals, three of 11 from three-point range, and six of eight at the foul line to end the night with 37 points. Hill had a double-double with 18 points and 13 rebounds, as well as Snow (13 points, 12 assists), and Mutombo (13 points, 11 rebounds). But the veteran Lakers were too strong to be denied a three-peat. The team made 45.1% of their total shots and three players had 20 or more points (O'Neal with 29, Bryant with 26, and Rich Fox with 20) to close out the series after just five games with a 108-96 win in front of a crushed 76ers crowd.

O'Neal averaged 33 points, 15 rebounds, and five assists for the series. Los Angeles also came through with clutch plays, and Philadelphia struggled to respond despite Iverson scoring 35 points or more in Game 3 through 5. But Philadelphia could take the moral victory in that they were the only 2001 NBA playoff team to draw blood on the Lakers. There were a lot of positive to take away from the season, and with fans seeing Iverson continue to improve on offense, they started to wonder what could the team do next year with a full year of a dominant rebounding player in Mutombo would do for the 76ers.

The Quick Fall, Early Playoff Exits

With the historic and incredible run that Allen Iverson put up for the Philadelphia 76ers during the postseason, one would only wonder how far he and his team could get in the following seasons. Was it simply just a fluke fueled by AI's competitive hunger? Was it simply a surprise run that teams in the East were not ready for? Or would Allen Iverson and the Philadelphia 76ers be legit contenders for years to come?

The answer turned out to be "not much." During the offseason, the 76ers lost starting power forward Tyrone Hill and Iverson underwent arthroscopic surgery on his right elbow. Iverson missed a combined total of 22 games during the season because of the injuries, and key players Aaron McKie and Eric Snow missed a combined 55 games. It was clear that the 76ers were not going to be the same team that they were the previous year.

Allen Iverson started the season on an on-and-off phase. There were nights where he would explode for big scoring games. Then, in between those performances were poor shooting games for The Answer. It was because Iverson had been suffering through injuries and was still recovering from surgery. He was the only source of offense. And despite his ailments, his team needed him to be there on the floor.

The first time Allen Iverson exploded for at least 40 points was when he had that number on November 28, 2001. He shot 15 out of 31 from the floor but had nine turnovers in what became a loss to the Washington Wizards. He then proceeded to score

30 points in each of the next two games as the 76ers struggled with inconsistency.

While Allen Iverson may have been hampered by injuries, he was still the league's premier scorer. On December 15, 2001, he would go for 40 points again when the Sixers won against the Cleveland Cavaliers. Following that performance, he torched the Boston Celtics two days later with 37 big points before going for 38 in a game against the Charlotte Hornets on December 19. The Philadelphia 76ers split both of those games.

It was not until January 7, 2002, when Allen Iverson logged in a triple-double. He would have 30 points, ten rebounds, and 11 assists in that huge 24-point win against the Los Angeles Clippers. Then, a little over a week later, The Answer would go for a new career game when the Philadelphia 76ers welcomed the Houston Rockets to town.

In a match that had to go to overtime for the 76ers to win, Allen Iverson was in sole possession of the ball in every play for Philadelphia. He would shoot 42 attempts from the floor. Those 42 attempts were nearly half of the 90 shots that the team put up. Nevertheless, AI would make 21 of those shots in addition to the 14 free throws he made. As the dust settled, he ended up with 58 big points. In contrast, the only other Sixer that scored in double digits was Speedy Claxton, who had 16. AI owned the offensive end as he accounted for more than half of the 112 points his team scored that night.

After that career high performance, Allen Iverson did not and could not slow down. He would go on to score at least 30 points in the next five games. This was capped off by the 47 points he put up in a win against the Boston Celtics on January 25, 2002. He made 16 of his 31 attempts from the floor while also draining 11 of his 13 free throw attempts.

Come March, Allen Iverson would have another run of incredible scoring performances. In a span of five games, AI would score 40 points in four of those outings. He started it off with 43 points in a win over the Nets on March 1, 2002. He then defeated the Raptors with his 42 points the following game. Sandwiching the two back-to-back 40-point games was his 28-point performance in a loss to Boston. After that, he would go for 46 and 41 points respectively against the Cavaliers and the Pacers on March 6 and 8. However, he would miss the few remaining weeks of the season due to injury.

While Iverson averaged 31 points per game and earned his third scoring title, he fell right back into his old habits of dominating the usage of the ball. This spurred further clashes between

Iverson and Larry Brown. Philadelphia went from winning 56 games and making it to the NBA Finals in 2001 to winning 43 games and losing in the first round in 2002. They lost in five games to the Boston Celtics and were thrashed in Game 5 120-87. Iverson averaged 30 points in the series, but only made 38.1% of the field goal attempts, averaging nearly 24 shot attempts in that first round.

Brown declared at the end-of-season press conference that he did not know if he could coach Philadelphia past the first round given Iverson's practice habits. Iverson responded with an infamous rant belittling practice where he used the word "practice" 23 times in less than three minutes. But what was often forgotten was how misunderstood and taken out of context AI was in that interview.

Allen Iverson had been missing practices in certain stretches of the previous season, but not because he was lazy or overconfident. He was licking and nursing wounds dealt by the death of his best friend Rahsaan Langford, who was shot and killed just before the season started. It was during the interview when the murder trial of Langford commenced. It opened deep wounds that Iverson had been trying to close throughout the season.[i]

It was never because Allen Iverson wanted to miss practice deliberately. He was never a lazy player. He was confident in himself, sometimes to a fault. But lazy was never a word to describe AI. He was a fighter, and he fought hard to get to where he was. He worked hard and exceeded the expectations that came with his small frame. But one could only wonder how far and how long AI was willing to fight as a lone star in Philadelphia. The 76ers needed to give him help soon.

Despite the ugly infighting that made national headlines, Iverson and Brown dealt with their differences and came together again for the 2002-2003 season. Philadelphia tried to get more offensive pieces around Iverson but traded key defensive players like Mutombo to get those pieces. More important than any trade was the fact that Iverson was back to being fully healthy.

He played all 82 games and no longer had to share the scoring burden quite so much as the 76ers were getting points throughout the starting five. A good example could be found on October 30, 2002, as the five starters all scored in double figures as Philadelphia defeated the Milwaukee Bucks, 95-93, at home. The 76ers were led by Iverson with 28 points and seven assists. McKie had 18 points, while newcomer Keith Van Horn had 16 points and eight rebounds. Two nights later, on

November 1, 2002, at home against the New York Knicks, Iverson converted 12 out of 30 field goals and 11 of 14 from the foul line to lead all players with 35 points in a 98-86 victory. Iverson would score another 34 points after making of 11 of 28 from the field and 12 of 15 free throws as the 76ers defeated the Los Angeles Clippers, 101-99.

Iverson would still have five games where he would score 40 or more points, even if he had some struggles with his jumper on a given night. That is because Iverson was so good at driving to the rim and getting fouled for free throw attempts and converting on those chances. One of the best examples of that was on February 21, 2003, when Iverson made 12 of 23 from the field (52.2%) and made 16 of 18 free throws. He finished the game with 41 points, six assists, and four steals to help Philadelphia get the 119-99 win on the road over the Cleveland Cavaliers.

On March 31, 2003, in Orlando, Florida, the 76ers defeated the Magic, 118-113, behind Iverson scoring 42 points to go along with six rebounds, six assists, and three steals in a game where he converted 15 of 31 total shots (48.4%) and another 10 of 14 free throws. Iverson would match that 42-point performance in a road game on April 15, 2003, making 11 of 28 field goals and 17 of 18 free throws in addition to eight rebounds, six assists,

69

and two steals. But the Bulls would win that game, 115-106, thanks to Jamal Crawford's 33 points and Eddy Curry with another 31 points as the team shot 63% from the field.

While Iverson was scoring a lot of points, he was not greedy like the past few seasons. As mentioned before, Iverson was being involved in distributing the offensive opportunities more to his teammates and that allowed him to have a career-high six double-doubles in the season that all came late in the season during the final playoff push.

On March 21, 2003, Iverson would have a season-high 12 assists to go along with 25 points in a 114-105 loss at home to the Atlanta Hawks. Despite the loss, five other teammates, including two players on the bench, had double digit points. After Iverson, Derrick Coleman had 17 points and ten rebounds in a double-double and Aaron McKie had 15 points from the bench.

That season-high assist numbers would be matched in a 108-101 win at home over the Chicago Bulls on April 2, 2003, as Iverson had 12 assists to go along with his 24 points from shooting 57.1% from the field. While Van Horn was second among the 76ers with 20 points, Kenny Thomas was the second star of the night as he had 16 points and 14 rebounds on 7 of 11

(63.6%) shooting that night. Overall, the team made 54.3 percent of their field goals in the win.

After the tough season one year ago, Philadelphia bounced back to win 48 games to barely fall short of claiming the Atlantic Division as the New Jersey Nets had 49 wins. The 76ers were still able to take the fourth seed and found themselves facing the fifth-seeded New Orleans Hornets (47-35) in a very interesting matchup that would go six games of the best of seven series for the first round of the Eastern Conference Playoffs. This was the first year of changing the first round from best of five to best of seven. With the home court advantage, Philadelphia would take the first two games, starting with a 98-90 victory on April 20, 2003. Iverson would lead all with a postseason career-high with 55 points after making 21 out of 32 field goals, including three out of five for three-pointers, for a 65.6 field goal percentage. He also added another eight assists and two steals in the game.

As a team, the 76ers were converting in the mid-40s for field goal percentage, and it continued in Game 2 on April 23, 2003, when they defeated the Hornets 90-85 while converting 44.6 % of their shots. Iverson led the team with 29 points, followed by the 17 points and 16 rebounds from Thomas. The entire starting five scored in double digits.

Iverson struggled in Game 3 on April 26, 2003, making only 34.5% of his shots and scoring 28 points in New Orleans. The other starters scored in double figures, but many of them struggled to get enough opportunities in a 99-85 loss. But that was only a small blip as they bounced back in Game 4 on April 28, 2003, with all six players finishing with double-digit scoring numbers. They were led by Iverson, who would score 22 points, followed by Eric Snow's 17 points and 12 assists. After a loss in Game 5 in Philadelphia, they were able to clinch the series in Game 6 on May 2, 2003, with a 107-103 win in New Orleans. Iverson had another big performance with 45 points after making 14 out of 30 field goals (46.7%), four of 10 from behind the three-point arc, and another 13 of 18 free throws. He also finished with seven rebounds, four assists, and two steals.

The next round was against the top-seeded Detroit Pistons, who finished 50-32 in the Central Division. During the first two games, the Pistons would win while Iverson was still strong, shooting 40 percent with 27 and 31 points, respectively. Philadelphia would take Games 3 and 4 in Philadelphia, starting with a 93-83 win on May 10, 2003, where Iverson struggled to get 25 points after only making 39.1% of his field goals. But the rest of the starting five were able to pick up in support with the other four starters scoring in double digits. Iverson would bounce back, at least for Game 4, on May 11, 2003, in a 95-82 win at home. He shot 48.1% from the field to finish with 36 points and 11 assists in a double-double.

Unfortunately, Iverson could not repeat that performance and Detroit would win Games 5 and 6. Iverson scored 14 points and 38 points, respectively, but he could have done better as he shot for only 32.8%. Detroit would advance to the Eastern Conference Finals before losing to the New Jersey Nets, who lost to the San Antonio Spurs. If that was not bad enough, Larry Brown was impressed with Detroit's defense. When Detroit let go of Coach Rick Carlisle in the 2003 offseason, Brown immediately grabbed the new coaching spot. It was the end of a tumultuous yet productive partnership between the coach wanting to play "the right way" and the shooting guard who played his way.

Despite the differences in opinions between the two icons, both Allen Iverson and Larry Brown maintained a healthy relationship. There was no bitterness between them. AI respected Brown just as well as how the latter learned how to respect and accept the former's style of play. Iverson would even, later on, claim that Larry Brown was the best coach in the world.

The Years of Struggles

The 2003-04 season would be an off year for Allen Iverson and the Philadelphia 76ers as they recovered from losing Larry Brown to the Pistons. Brown would be replaced by Randy Ayers, who would fail to form a bond of respect that made Allen Iverson and his previous coach close. It was going to be a short stint for Ayers and the troubled Sixers.

With the new coaching system in place, Allen Iverson would fail to lead his team by his lonesome unlike how did in previous years. But even with his failure to become the one-man wrecking crew he used to be under Brown, Iverson started the season well on a personal note. He would score at least 30 points five times in his first ten games. This included a night where he had 40 in a win over the Washington Wizards on November 11, 2003. He followed it up with 36 points versus the Spurs a few nights later.

On November 29, AI would explode for 50 big points in a win against the Atlanta Hawks. He made 20 of his 34 shots from the field along with four from the three-point area. After that game, he would score 35 points three consecutive times against the Raptors, the Bulls, and the Heat. He went 2-1 in those three great performances.

While Allen Iverson may have been hot in the early part of the season, he would be forced to sit out a bunch of games because of nagging injuries in his right knee. He had been using so much of his explosive speed and quickness that it took a toll on his body. That and the 40 minutes per night he had been playing since his rookie season added up to the wear and tear of carrying a franchise as a lone star.

Iverson would make a return from injury on January 5, 2004, after nearly a month of absence. He scored only 18 points in that loss to the Milwaukee Bucks. This was also the time when Iverson had been feuding with new head coach Chris Ford, who tried a disciplinarian approach on Iverson. He would suspend his superstar a few games then and there because of AI's alleged disciplinary issues. Iverson would fail to inform his team about getting sick and would even miss practices. The Answer would even feel insulted that Ford once wanted him to come off the bench after returning from injury. Safe to say, that relationship was also short-lived.

Allen Iverson's season would end abruptly on March 20, 2004, after nagging knee injuries continued to bother him throughout the year. However, that did not stop him from making another All-Star appearance and from averaging 26.4 points, 3.7 rebounds, and 6.8 assists. He would miss a total of 34 games that season because of all the injuries and disciplinary measures. The Sixers failed to make the playoffs.

The following season, a new head coach by the name of Jim O'Brien tried to steer the ship back to its right direction. The Sixers would also acquire new key pieces like first round draft pick Andre Iguodala and former All-Star Chris Webber, who was acquired midseason via a trade. Sophomore shooter Kyle Korver also manned the wings ready to hit open jumpers. But the biggest asset remained to be Allen Iverson, who recovered well from his knee injuries.

A healthier AI was not merely a scorer that season. Being the ball dominant player that he was, he was also dishing out assists at a career rate. He would have his first double-double of the season on November 9, 2004, when he went for 29 points and ten assists in a loss to the New York Knicks. He would have five double-doubles through his first 12 games of the season.

On December 12, 2004, Allen Iverson would go for a rare high-scoring double-double in a win against the Milwaukee Bucks. He had 40 points and ten assists that game after going for 22 points and ten assists two nights before that. He would even have a near triple-double in the next game after he finished the win against the Denver Nuggets with 31 points, ten rebounds, and eight assists. Often regarded as a selfish player, AI was showing that he could be a great distributor as long as he had the ball in his hands.

In the middle of December, Allen Iverson would even go for a rare feat of recording back-to-back games of scoring over 50 points. He started with the 54 he had in Milwaukee on December 18, 2004. He made 17 of his 29 shots from the floor and 16 of his 21 free throw attempts. Iverson followed that up two nights later by going for 51 points in a loss to the Utah Jazz. He made 18 of his 31 shots that game. And with the 40 points he put up in a win against the Indiana Pacers in the next match, he racked up a total of 145 points in a span of only three games.

On January 24, 2005, AI went for another rare high-scoring double-double performance after going for 45 points and ten assists in a win against the Miami Heat. He finished with three double-doubles in the last five games that he played. And over the course of the next five games, he would go for three double-doubles again. This was an Allen Iverson intent on making use of his passing skills as well.

Though Iverson was making sure he was also becoming a facilitator, he did not deviate from his natural instinct—scoring the ball. On February 12, 2005, AI would go for a new career high of 60 points in a win over the Orlando Magic. He ran circles around the defense by converting 17 of his 36 shots. He would also go on to sink 24 of his 27 free throw attempts for that incredible scoring outburst.

March was also one of Allen Iverson's biggest months that season. In that month alone, he scored above 30 points in all but four of 16 games he played. He never even went lower than 25 points during March 2005. He was simply as good a scorer as anyone could find in the history of the NBA. You almost even forget that he is barely 6 feet tall while other players that have accomplished the same feat were a lot bigger than he was.

As the dust settled, it was a bounce-back season for Allen Iverson, who once again led the league in scoring for the fourth and final time in his career. Together with George Gervin, Iverson had reached third place all-time in most scoring titles won. Only Kevin Durant has led the league in scoring four times since then. Michael Jordan, with ten scoring titles, remains untouched in that category.

AI would norm 30.7 points, four rebounds, 7.9 assists (career high), and 2.4 steals the entire season. He also shot a then-career best of 83.5% from the free throw line. Iverson would also lead the Philadelphia 76ers back to the playoffs with a record of 43-

39 under Jim O'Brien. However, his team would easily be defeated in five games by the Larry Brown coached Detroit Pistons in the first round. Iverson scored at least 30 points in all but Game 2 of that series.

For the 2005-06 season, adjustments had to be made again after O'Brien was fired due to clashes with personnel and players. A 76er legend of old, Maurice Cheeks, took over the helm as the new head coach. Like others before him, Cheeks gave Iverson full reigns over the offense of the Philadelphia 76ers. Iverson rightfully took advantage of it as he was once again trying to get his team back to the Promised Land.

Iverson, like always, started the season on a good scoring note having scored above 30 points in 14 tries in his first 20 games of the season. Those 14 games included five outings of scoring at least 40. His high at that time was the 45 points he scored in a loss to the Milwaukee Bucks on November 23, 2005. The lowest he scored at that point of the season were only 23 points. It was becoming clear that he was gunning for his fifth scoring title.

On December 23, 2005, Allen Iverson broke the 50-point barrier for the first time that season. In that loss to Atlanta, he made 17 of his 31 shots and 19 of his 21 free throw attempts.

Iverson would end the game with a total of 53 points. Those 53 points were the most that Allen Iverson could muster up that season. Nevertheless, he stayed consistent all year long by figuring himself above 30 points for the majority of the season.

On January 9 and 11, AI would go for back-to-back 40-point games. He first had 41 points on 15 out of 25 shooting from the field in a win against the Seattle SuperSonics before going for 46 points on 16 out of 25 shooting from the field in a loss to the Utah Jazz. He would go for 33 points and ten assists in the next game, which was a win against the Boston Celtics.

Allen Iverson would go for a season high of 15 assists on top of the 38 points he scored when the Philadelphia 76ers lost to the Orlando Magic on January 26. That was one game after he went for 41 big points in a win against the Sacramento Kings. AI, however, would miss a few games after that because of minor injuries. He would make his return on February 4 to score 34 points like it was nothing in a win against the Cleveland Cavaliers.

Shortly after making his seventh consecutive All-Star appearance, Iverson would mount back-to-back 40-10 double-doubles on points and assists. The first was on March 1 when he had 40 points and ten dimes in a win against the Houston

Rockets. He followed that up with 47 points and 12 assists when the Sixers defeated the Washington Wizards.

By the end of the season, the then 30-year-old veteran scoring guard had averaged a career high 33 points along with 7.4 assists. The high scoring total was a function of the league and career high 43 minutes per game he played that season. Despite tallying his best scoring season, Iverson failed to win the scoring title for a fifth time because Kobe Bryant was going off in Los Angeles by averaging 35 points thanks to the numerous scoring outbursts (which included an 81-point game) he had that season. Despite his gaudy numbers, AI was only Third Team All-NBA. His team failed to make the postseason again.

Chapter 6: The Later Years in Denver, Detroit, and Memphis

The Trade to the Denver Nuggets, Teaming Up With Carmelo Anthony

Even before the season got started, there were already reports that the Philadelphia 76ers and Allen Iverson were beginning to see reasons to part ways. Rumors circulated that the Denver Nuggets, Atlanta Hawks, and the Boston Celtics were all interested in the services of the four-time scoring leader. But none of the trades materialized, and Allen Iverson returned to Philadelphia for the following season.

However, Iverson's return to the Sixers for the 2006-07 season was short-lived. After playing only 15 games, he was so disappointed and frustrated with how management handled the roster that it was reported that he demanded a trade. Owner Ed Snider confirmed the trade rumors, believing that the relationship was not working anymore. He would not play in any more games after the trade demand.

Iverson was the face of the Philadelphia 76ers since 1996. He may have had a bad boy image because of his hair, tattoos, and the way he dressed. Nevertheless, he was a cultural icon that looked as erratic and flamboyant as he was on the hardwood floor where he let his game do the talking. Iverson had poured his heart out for the Philadelphia 76ers to muster up the highest scoring average of 28.1 points for the team in those ten years. He also ranked second all-time in most points scored as a Sixer.

Perhaps the most memorable part of Allen Iverson's tenure as a member of the Philadelphia 76ers was when he was essentially a one-man show in dragging the team all the way to the 2001 NBA Finals to steal one game from the eventual dominant champions. He was the MVP that season, and his performance in the Finals was a testament to how great he was all year long. But while the rest of his stay in Philadelphia had been marred with criticisms, broken relationships, alleged selfish and lazy tendencies, Iverson was the entire 76ers franchise. Without him, the Sixers would have been a laughing stock in the league.

On December 19, 2006, Allen Iverson was traded to the Denver Nuggets. The Denver Nuggets would give up pass-first point guard Andre Miller and Joe Smith along with several draft picks for the services of one of the greatest scorers to have ever played the game. Oddly enough, the Nuggets also had their great young scorer waiting in the wings to one day follow suit to what AI had accomplished.

Denver already had an elite isolation scorer in Carmelo Anthony, and there were concerns about how well Carmelo and Iverson could work together. After all, Allen Iverson has never played with a fellow great scorer his entire career. He has had the chance to play alongside former All-Stars, but never ones that were at the peak of their careers. This was a challenge not only to AI but the rest of the Nuggets organization.

Fortunately, Coach George Karl had a long reputation of creating excellent offenses. Iverson no longer dominated the ball as often as he did, being the lone star of the 76ers, but that meant he could pick and choose his spots. In his first game wearing the blue and gold of the Nuggets, Iverson played as a reserve and converted 9 out of 15 field goals to score 22 points and collect 10 assists on December 22, 2006. It was an impressive individual performance despite resulting in a 101-96 loss to the Sacramento Kings at home in Denver's Pepsi Center.

Iverson followed that up with a 116-105 home win over the Boston Celtics on December 26, 2006, where Iverson started and scored 28 points and collected 13 assists. It did not take long until Iverson would have a high scoring game as he made 17 out of 29 field goals (58.6%) to finish with 44 points and ten assists in his third straight double-double in a 112-98 win over the Seattle SuperSonics on December 28, 2006.

Adjusting to Carmelo Anthony was not easy, but AI did it well by knowing when to shoot and when to pass off to find others who had better shots. On one night, it was Allen Iverson playing the role of the usual high scorer the world had come to love and admire. But on other nights, he was a facilitator that loved nothing more than to get his teammates going on the scoring end. This was shown by the 36 points and ten assists he had in an overtime win against the Houston Rockets on January 20, 2007.

Allen Iverson's penchant for making plays took another step higher when he had three consecutive double-doubles in the middle of March. On March 13, he would go for 31 points and ten assists against the Portland Trailblazers. He followed that up with 14 points and 13 dimes against the Lakers before ending the streak with his then-Denver Nuggets high of 44 points alongside his season high of 15 assists versus the Phoenix Suns. All three games were wins.

During his 50 games with the Nuggets, Iverson shot more than 45% in his first season, which was a number he had not had since his sophomore year, and scored 25 points per game. He also became a better passer, averaging roughly the same amount of assists even though he now had the ball less often.

While Anthony and Iverson was a strong offensive pair, the Nuggets lacked a defensive core. It was a team predicated on the elite level offense of both of their star players. However, the Nuggets won 45 games and made the playoffs as the eighth seed in the much more competitive Western Conference. The East is known for having at least one team below .500 to earn a lower seed into the playoffs. The West was a lot different. The most elite teams in the NBA play in that conference. After ten years of staying in the East, Iverson would have a taste of how truly wild the West was.

It looked like the Nuggets would have a good team considering they defeated the favored San Antonio Spurs with a 95-89 win on April 22, 2007, in Game 1 of their first-round matchup. Iverson made 11 out 22 field goals and all eight free throws to finish with 31 points, while Anthony was right behind him with 10 out of 18 field goals (55.6%) and made all eight of his free throws for 30 points.

Anthony and Iverson would score 26 and 20 with less than 40% efficiency from the field between them in a Game 2 loss, 97-88 on April 25, 2007. They had similar numbers throughout the rest of the series, and the Spurs would take in five games. However, there was a lot of hope in them in Denver.

Second and Final Full Season with the Denver Nuggets

Iverson completely rejuvenated himself for the 2007-2008 season. For the first time since the 2002-2003 season, he had no nagging injuries and played all 82 games. Again, Iverson and Anthony played well together and created one of the best 1-2 scoring punches in the NBA. The supporting cast also improved. Often injured All-Star power forward, Kenyon Martin, played 71 games after playing just two in 2006-2007, and young shooting guard, JR Smith, likewise developed into a capable scorer.

With the amount of scorers surrounding the core duo of Allen Iverson and Carmelo Anthony, it was a stark contrast to what the four-time scoring champion had been suffering from early in his career. He was a lone scoring threat surrounded by defensive talent. He hardly had any offensive help around him when he was in Philadelphia. The Denver Nuggets made sure that the same would not happen.

But even though Allen Iverson had a lot of capable scorers around him, he was nevertheless still one of the better players in putting up points on the board. He would begin the season with 25 points, 14 assists, and seven steals in a win against the

Seattle SuperSonics. He proceeded to score above 20 points in the next four games of the early part of the season.

After mostly figuring himself a little over 20 points in that juncture of the season, Iverson had a season-high of 51 points converting 18 out of 27 field goals (66.7%) and another 15 of 18 at the foul line on December 5, 2007, in a 111-107 loss in Denver. He also had eight assists during the game. Anthony had 26 points in his game, and their big man Marcus Camby led the team with 20 rebounds without any points.

The Nuggets would bounce right back the very next night on December 6, 2007, in a 122-109 win in Dallas where Iverson had another efficient night on offense where he made 12 out of 29 field goals (63.2%) and 11 of 13 free throws to finish with 35 points. Allen Iverson would also finish that game with 12 assists and six steals. Anthony would score 23 points of his own in that match.

After that win against the Dallas Mavericks, Iverson would then have double-doubles on points and assists in the next two games, which were both wins for the Denver Nuggets. He had 23 points and ten assists against the Sacramento Kings. After that, he would finish a win against the New Orleans Hornets with 22 points and 11 assists.

During the month of December, Allen Iverson would have seven games of scoring above 30 points. This included the previously mentioned night where he had 51. He also had four consecutive outings of tallying above 30 markers. He started with 30 points in a loss to the Spurs. Following that, he had 38 in another loss. This time it was against the Portland Trailblazers. He then combined for 70 points in an overtime win against the Houston Rockets and a loss to Portland again.

Because he was not the only scoring threat, Iverson did not have to take the majority of the field goal attempts like he did for years in Philadelphia. As previously mentioned, that allowed him to pick his spots, and he did not have to force shots that had less chance of going in. In fact, Iverson had five games where he had at least 70 percent from the field.

On February 8, 2008, Iverson only took nine field goal attempts but made seven of them (77.8 percent) and four out of five free throws to score 18 points. His 11 assists also helped his teammates. Anthony was the lead scorer with 49 points in that game, and he also shot 76 percent from the field. Later in the month on February 27, 2008, Iverson made 13 out of 18 field goals (72.2%), with three of five from behind the three-point arc to score 31 points in a 138-96 win in Seattle. Seven other

Nuggets scored in double figures and made 67% of their total field goal attempts.

On March 19, 2008, Iverson finally returned to Philadelphia to play against his old team. He said that it was good to be back, hugged his past teammates, and kissed the Sixers logo on the court. Even though Iverson and the 76ers had not left on the best terms, he knew how much he had done for them, and vice versa. Iverson would put up 32 points and eight assists in his old stomping grounds. It was the Sixers that ended up with the win.

He was also having a better season passing the ball and distributing the offensive opportunities to Anthony and other Denver teammates. He also had a career-high of 15 double-doubles in the season. The 586 assists on the season were the most since nearly having 600 in the 2004-2005 season, and the majority of his career would show him getting less than 400 in a year.

It was a career year of endurance for Iverson, who would lead the league with an average of 41.8 minutes per game while scoring 26.4 points per game on 45.8% shooting along with seven assists and three rebounds. Although the 2000-2001 season was the time when Iverson became a full-fledged star, some metrics show that the 2007-2008 season was, in fact, the best of his career.

The Nuggets improved and won 50 games in 2007-2008, but unfortunately, the rest of the Western Conference had improved as well. Despite the higher win total, Denver was once again the eighth seed in an extremely competitive Western Conference.

In the first round of the NBA Playoffs, the Nuggets found themselves pitted against the Los Angeles Lakers, who were at the top again with a 57-25 record. The Lakers had a potent one-two punch of the MVP Kobe Bryant and All-Star big man Pau Gasol. It was evident that the West had a lot of good teams when all eight teams in the conference playoffs are within seven games of each other.

While the Nuggets looked like a strong team, the Lakers were able to make a four-game sweep to advance en route to another trip to the NBA Finals where they eventually lost in six games to the Boston Celtics. During those four games, Iverson averaged 24.5 points per game while making 43.4% from the field, while Anthony struggled, by his standards, with 22.5 points per game and shot 36.4% from the field.

The Trade to the Detroit Pistons, the Start of the Fall

After only three games in the 2008-2009 season, Iverson was abruptly traded to the Detroit Pistons for Chauncey Billups. The deal came as a mutual decision that favored both the Detroit Pistons and Denver Nuggets. The Pistons, with new executive Joe Dumars, wanted a shakeup in the roster that had been intact ever since winning the 2004 NBA Championship. The Denver Nuggets, on the other hand, wanted a real point guard to man the plays.

Iverson himself was excited about the trade. It was not because he disliked playing for the Nuggets, but because he wanted to prove he could play in a systematic franchise. The Pistons also wanted Iverson solely because he gave them a new offensive dimension. Dumars thought that the Pistons had failed to repeat as champions because they were becoming too predictable. Allen Iverson was their answer for that predictability.

The Pistons had made the Eastern Conference Finals for the past six years, and Iverson was initially excited to be part of a winning team. Furthermore, the Eastern Conference at the time was not as difficult as the Western Conference where 50 games only earned Denver the eighth seed and a four-game sweep to the Los Angeles Lakers. However, Iverson quickly realized upon his arrival that Detroit was, instead, looking to rebuild. They had not traded for Iverson's basketball skills but for the fact that, unlike Billups, Iverson was in the last year of a big contract.

Detroit planned to bench Iverson and let the young guard, Rodney Stuckey, develop. Then, they would use the money they saved and trade Iverson to get a big free agent in the 2009 offseason. The proud Iverson played hard at first, but as Stuckey got more and more playing time, Iverson ferociously objected to the idea that he should be placed on the bench. He claimed that the Detroit front office had promised him they would never do that and said later in the season to the *New York Times* that he would rather retire than serve as a bench player.

While Allen Iverson would rarely play off the bench as a Piston, his role was not as significant as it was in his last two teams. The Detroit Pistons relied on a slow-paced offensive style that focused on using different players for their offensive needs. That did not fit well into Allen Iverson's isolation style of play. And despite playing huge minutes for the Pistons, his shot attempts were limited as he could not adjust well to the new system, though he would make the All-Star Game again mainly due to his popularity.

Shortly afterward, Pistons general manager, Joe Dumars, said that Iverson was done for the season after he played in Detroit's 111-98 loss in New Jersey on April 1, 2009, where he only made one of eight field goals in 17 minutes off the bench. It was becoming too obvious that Allen Iverson was not meant to be a Piston and was better off doing his thing for another team.

Iverson played just 54 games and averaged 17.4 points and 4.9 assists per game during that season. While the Pistons made the playoffs, the former scoring champion and league MVP did not play or even attend the games as LeBron James' Cleveland Cavaliers ignominiously swept the Pistons. The free agents that the Pistons signed in the 2009 offseason turned out to become complete disasters, and Detroit has not made the playoffs for a long while since then.

At that point, Iverson's career was essentially over. He signed with the Memphis Grizzlies in the 2009-2010 season. However, once again, he clashed with the management's decision of him coming off the bench. In three games playing with the Grizzlies, he averaged just 12.3 points per game and playing for only about 22 minutes per game, shooting 58% from the field. Memphis coach, Lionel Hollins, ordered Iverson to conform to the team philosophy or face the consequences. Iverson refused to comply and parted ways with Memphis after playing for just three games.

At first, Iverson contemplated retirement. However, three weeks later, he signed a contract to return to the Philadelphia 76ers. On Iverson's first game as a returning 76er, he was received with raucous applause from the Philadelphia fans as they hosted another former team of Iverson, the Denver Nuggets, on December 7, 2009. The Nuggets would prevail with a 93-83 win. In this game, Iverson made only four out of 11 field goals for a total of 11 points. The team had some other players who were used to the system that head coach, Eddie Jordan, put in place with players like Andre Iguodala, who made 31 points.

It was the worst season for Iverson concerning statistics as he failed to score anywhere close to the 30-point mark. His highest scoring game was on January 29, 2010, in a 99-91 loss at home to the Los Angeles Lakers. Iverson scored 23 points after making 10 out of 18 field goals (55.6%). After only 25 games with the 76ers, his time with the team ended in less than amicable ways despite both parties sharing so many good memories in the late 1990s and early 2000s. That season, Iverson was only at 13.8 points per game, averaging four assists and less than three rebounds per game. In previous seasons when he played with Denver and Detroit, Iverson never had less than 22 points per game. In the years before that, he even had an average of 30 or more points during his highlight years.

He continued to linger around the fringes of the NBA for a few more years. He signed a two-year contract worth $4 million with a team in the Turkish Basketball League, which was on the second level of professional basketball in Europe with the press conference held in New York City on October 29, 2010. In his debut with Beşiktaş on November 16, 2010, he scored 15 points in 23 minutes in a 94-91 loss to Hemofarm from Serbia. After playing ten games with the Turkish club, Iverson returned to the US in 2011 to have calf surgery.

Two years later in January 2013, Iverson received an offer to play for the Texas Legends, a team that is part of the NBA's Development League, better known as the D-League. Soon after, Iverson realized that his time playing professional basketball was over and he officially retired in October 2013. In a public press conference, he said that he did not have the drive to try and get back on a basketball court. It was an unfortunate ending for one of the greatest players in NBA history.

Chapter 7: Days After Retirement

Celebrated NBA players have always enjoyed getting the fans' star treatment in the twilight years of their careers. Knowing that the star's retirement was nearing, fans would savor the final games of the NBA player's last season as they might never see such greatness again on the hardwood floor. This was a recurring theme in the NBA.

Celebrated NBA legends such as Michael Jordan and Kobe Bryant have all received ovations from opposing crowds during the twilight years of their respective careers. For Jordan, he went out with a bang in his second retirement as a Bull in 1998. He would win the NBA title in his final game that season. Then, in 2003, he would spend the entire season as a rock star playing against opposing teams. This was the same treatment that Kobe Bryant had when he announced his retirement in 2015. He spent the entire season parading and getting cheered on by other teams.

On the other hand, while some players were not able the received the rock star parade and status that guys like Jordan and Kobe had when they were retiring, they nonetheless ended their final seasons on a good note. Tim Duncan, the best power forward in league history, finished his NBA career by making the second round of the playoffs. Shaquille O'Neal spent his final days moving from one team to another, but helped those teams contend for playoff positions. And legendary point guard Jason Kidd won a title in one of his final seasons before going over to help a struggling franchise like the New York Knicks.

But things were different for Allen Iverson. Fans may have loved him, but there were no rock star parades or adorations from opposing arenas and fellow stars. He slowly died into the night after getting traded to the Pistons. Essentially no team wanted to sign for his services though he still had a lot of fuel left in him. He became an irrelevant free agent because of his brash attitude and penchant for going against authority.

But those qualities were what made Allen Iverson himself. He was a legend precisely because of his brashness and specifically because he went against odds. He was indifferent to the opinions of the media, coaches, general managers, executives, and fellow players themselves. He was an alpha star that did not try hard enough to be a star. He was a star because his attitude made him so. Iverson's style of play and refusal to give in made him the biggest star of his era without even trying to be.

And while Allen Iverson may have been the greatest star during the early 2000's, his star fell low even before the dawn of the new decade. He was only 35 years old, but his game and his personality refused to adjust just the same as he refused to be limited by his physical attributes. At his age, he could no longer blow past defenders or run the fast break in only seconds. At his size, he could not contend with the bigger, faster, and younger guards. And with his personality, Allen Iverson was not seen as a veteran that could spark inspiration in younger players.

Allen Iverson was always a lone star from his days in Georgetown up to his stardom in Philadelphia. Even in Denver, he acted like a lone star despite playing with the likes of Carmelo Anthony and several other capable scorers. He was a solo act, but that was what made him unique and great. He was a polarizing figure in the NBA. It was either you loved him or despised him. Unfortunately, coaches and teams disliked him at that point in his career. Nobody saw his worth despite the great moments and accomplishments he achieved in his career. His phone was silent. Nobody gave him a call. Allen Iverson was done as far as professional basketball was concerned.

After his professional basketball years, Allen Iverson did not handle retirement well. He saw financial problems at that point in his life despite the many millions he made from his contracts in the NBA and from the endorsement's he has had in an illustrious career. But even with his problems, Allen Iverson remained a loved figure in Philadelphia.

Allen Iverson's number 3 jersey as a Sixer would be retired by the franchise he played for in the first ten years of his career. The ceremony happened on March of 2014. A crowd of 20,000 people, which was a rarity for the struggling Sixers at that time, cheered on to give their adoration to the franchise's most iconic player. His jerseys were being sold for a hefty sum, but nobody cared. It was the final moment that Allen Iverson would have for his beloved Philadelphia 76ers, and everyone in the city knew that. His name and jersey number would be raised up to the rafters together with all-time NBA legends such as Julius Erving, Maurice Cheeks, Wilt Chamberlain, and Charles Barkley.

Early in 2017, it was announced that Allen Iverson would be among some of the retired NBA All-Stars that would take part in an all-new 3-on-3 league for former professional basketball players. Popular celebrity Ice Cube founded the new league.[ii] Cube wanted to watch his favorite basketball players duke it out once more on the hard floor. That was one of the reasons why he had to form such a league.

In an interview, Allen Iverson said that he did not hesitate to accept the offer. He loved Ice Cube and thought it was a no-brainer to accept such a decision given the man's star status in Hollywood. Knowing how successful of a celebrity Ice Cube was, Allen Iverson wanted to be a big part of the impending success that was the 3-on-3 league. Iverson expressed that he would put in a lot of effort to make the league a success, just like how he put his heart on the line every single night in the NBA.[ii]

Among the other former NBA players that were alleged to have expressed their commitment to the league are Kenyon Martin, Chauncey Billups, and Stephen Jackson. Players with less star value such as Rashard Lewis, Jermaine O'Neal, Jason Williams, and Mike Bibby have also expressed their desire to commit to the new venture.

While Allen Iverson would serve as a coach in the new league, it was also announced that he would also take part as a player. Among the other coaches announced are Gary Payton and George Gervin. It was also at the time of the announcement when Allen Iverson was questioned again about his famous practice rant. He would joke about it and say that he would not have reached the heights he has achieved if he did not practice.

Chapter 8: Iverson's Personal Life

As great as Iverson was on the basketball court, it was the things off the court that defined him for both good and bad. Iverson had a tough life, having been forced to battle the law in a trial which some argued had racist undertones, and having been doubted for his temperament as early as middle school. In addition to his renegade status, Iverson's small height as compared to the behemoths of most NBA players, contributed to his underdog image. The little man of the NBA represented the ordinary men of the world.

Iverson did not represent the little men of the world by being one of them, but by being what they dreamed of being. He revolutionized fashion both inside and outside the NBA. In the 2000-2001 season, Iverson injured his right elbow, and so he began to wear an elbow sleeve to protect it, which was a nylon accessory which covered most of his arm. The elbow sleeve quickly became popular among NBA players. It was not because the sleeve was proven effective at stopping injuries, but because even NBA players wanted a piece of Iverson's swagger. Today, LeBron James wears an elbow sleeve on his right elbow, and Carmelo Anthony wears a sleeve on each elbow. Iverson also popularized the headband, another favorite item among basketball players today. In fact, the influence has spread beyond the NBA. If you walk into any pick-up basketball game, there is a good chance that someone on that court will be wearing either an elbow sleeve or a headband.

Off the basketball court, Iverson was crucial to connecting the world of hip-hop to basketball. Hip-hop and basketball have always shared connections as a means for young black men to escape rough neighborhoods, but Iverson helped popularize and bring the combination into the mainstream. Iverson partied with rappers, partied like a rapper, and routinely wore clothes straight from hip-hop fashion. Iverson's shoe deals with Reebok also emphasized the hip-hop world. For example, the commercial for the A5 and A6 shoes both used American rapper Jadakiss, who rapped about Iverson's incredible basketball talent. When Iverson was injured and spent time on the Philadelphia bench during games, he routinely showed up wearing sports jerseys, metal chains, and other styles from hip-hop fashion. Just like Iverson was a trendsetter for elbow sleeves and headbands, he became a trendsetter for off-court fashion. In fact, other basketball players began to wear similar clothing.

However, there were those who opposed such style, especially NBA Commissioner, David Stern. Stern believed that if the influence of hip-hop on basketball grew too strong, it would turn off the NBA's dominantly white fanbase. Consequently, in 2005, Stern implemented a dress code for NBA players sitting on the bench. Hip-hop apparel such as chains and baggy shorts were banned and replaced by dress shirts and slacks. Iverson explicitly stated his opposition to the ban and said that Stern had gone overboard. While the dress code continues to be enforced to this day, the fact that Stern went so far as to implement a ban shows just how much Iverson could influence those inside and outside the NBA to follow his example of being the fearless rebel.

Not all of Iverson's impacts on the NBA was positive. Iverson was never interested in backing down from a challenge off the court than on the court, which has led to trouble throughout his career. He was accused of having a gambling and drinking addiction. In fact, Iverson has been banned from multiple casinos, and there were many stories about how Iverson could go broke due to his lifestyle. While it is a sad truth that many athletes go broke after their professional careers are over, that is not the case with Iverson. With his contract with Reebok, Iverson will continue to have a reliable income for the rest of his life. Nevertheless, this fact did not prevent the stories regarding Iverson's financial troubles from going around.

Perhaps there are those unwilling to accept that a man like Iverson, who refused to play by the rules, and lived an openly black, hip-hop lifestyle, could not end up in tragedy. However, after all that Iverson had been through, including the incredible difficulties he experienced in life, he is one person who deserves a happy ending.

Chapter 9: Impact on Basketball

Iverson may have an unparalleled legacy when it came to his brand and how he fused hip-hop and basketball. But what exactly was Iverson's impact on basketball? This question seems to be complicated to answer. Iverson scored a great deal. In fact, he was the NBA scoring champion four times, and the third-most alongside George Gervin and Kevin Durant. Over the course of 14 seasons in the NBA, Iverson would have a total of 24,368 points for an average of 26.7 per game and shooting 42.5% of his field goals. 31.3% of these came from behind the three-point line, and throughout his career, he played in a total of more than 900 games. The rest of his career statistic line showed that Iverson would have averages of 6.2 assists, 3.7 rebounds, and 2.2 steals. However, did those huge amounts of points translated into wins, or did Iverson just use up immense amounts of possessions to improve his individual numbers at the expense of the team?

In discussing Iverson's legacy as a basketball player, the first thing to do is to not talk about Iverson, but rather the players around him. On the one hand, Iverson had to carry a mediocre supporting cast for years. He never played alongside a single All-Star in his ten years with the Philadelphia 76ers. As noted above, Iverson averaged 31.1 points per game when he led the 2001 76ers squad to the NBA Finals. Only one other player who was with Philadelphia the entire season averaged double digits in points – Aaron McKie, who only scored 11 points per game. It, thus, appears to be obvious that Iverson carried that mediocre supporting cast to the NBA Finals with his incredible scoring ability.

However, there is an alternative explanation for the 2001 76ers. The players around Iverson were poor scorers but excellent defenders. Iverson may not have played alongside an All-Star, but he did play alongside Dikembe Mutombo, who won the Defensive Player of the Year Award in 2001. Eric Snow and Aaron McKie were good defenders, and Larry Brown is one of the best defensive coaches in the history of the league. After Brown had left the 76ers, he coached the Detroit Pistons to become the best defensive team of the 2000s and later brought the Charlotte Bobcats to the playoffs with a stout defense. Furthermore, from 1998 to 2002, when the 76ers achieved their biggest playoff success in the Iverson years, they were consistently a top five defensive team. Some assert that instead of Iverson carrying a mediocre supporting cast; it was the supporting cast with their stalwart defense that carried Iverson.

Iverson's legacy is also quite controversial. Despite his incredible scoring prowess, the 76ers and Denver Nuggets did not get particularly worse when he left. Philadelphia won 38 games in 2005-2006, Iverson's last full season with the team. Then, they won 35 games in 2006-07, the season he was traded to Denver, and 40 games in 2007-2008. The Denver Nuggets improved when they traded Iverson for a more traditional point guard in Chauncey Billups. They won 54 games in 2008-2009 and reached the Western Conference Finals after losing in the first round the past two years with Iverson. On the other side of the coin, Iverson found himself on struggling teams in Detroit and Memphis before finishing his NBA career in the familiar Philadelphia uniform.

In addition to the discussion about how teams were built around Iverson as well as how much better or worse they got when he was on the floor, one can criticize aspects of his individual game beyond the well-known fact that he held the ball too much. Iverson was never a great three-point shooter and never shot more than 35% from the three-point line at any point in his career. Being a poor three-point shooter is not an irredeemable weakness, but Iverson exacerbated this problem by shooting many three-point shots. He shot four three-pointers per game as a 76er, but made less than 31% of them. Furthermore, while no one can accuse Iverson of being a lazy defender, he was significantly limited by his small frame. Iverson, however, stole the ball a great deal, averaging over two for his career but he played the passing lanes to get those steals and gambled. When the gamble failed, his team's defense would be forced to play 4 on 5 for a brief moment, which frequently led to easy baskets.

There may be plenty of criticisms in Iverson's career, yet basketball is more than just a game of numbers. It is a game of heart and will where lesser players can defeat greater players if they work hard enough. While there were players in Iverson's time who were undoubtedly better than him, none of them cared about winning every single game more than Iverson. Iverson's dedication was not just about himself, but also about inspiring his teammates to do all they could to secure a victory.

Even if Iverson may have held the ball too often, the way in which he played showed how much he cared about winning. Iverson was famous for his crossover and dribble moves and step-back jumpers. But Iverson's bread and butter was not a fancy, difficult jumper. It was to charge into the paint, surrounded by giants over a foot taller and a hundred pounds heavier than he was over and over again. His style involved scoring layups, draw hard fouls, and hit the ground to get right back up. Iverson did this game after game, year after year until his body could no longer handle it. He never cared about the pain. As long as he could win, that intense fire of his continued to burn long after his body could not handle it. If anything, Iverson would be known best as one of the scrappiest six-foot-tall players who was fearless enough to play like he was as big as some of the best who defended the paint. He was like a small dog, which may not be as big as the other dog in a fight, but he was, at the very least, going to put up the biggest fight. Iverson's teammates loved him for it, which puts into question the claim that Iverson killed team chemistry. Eric Snow declared that he loved Allen Iverson and Dikembe Mutombo said that Iverson "had something burning inside him that made him unstoppable."

In addition to what Iverson meant to the 76ers, he had a significant impact on the NBA as a whole. As noted above, his repertoire of crossovers and dribble moves inspired millions to try his same moves on the basketball court, including future NBA players. But Iverson, in fact, did not represent a new phase, but rather a culmination. In the aftermath of Michael Jordan's six championships, many NBA general managers attempted to find a "new Jordan," a new shooting guard skilled in the isolation who could win games. Iverson was far from the only shooting guard in the late 1990s to the early 2000s who was expected to carry his team single-handedly to victory. New York had Allan Houston, Houston had Steve Francis, Orlando had Penny Hardaway, Charlotte had Baron Davis, and so on. However, Iverson was the best among these guards.

Moreover, Jordan was unique. What basketball management failed to understand was that what worked for Jordan does not necessarily work for another shooting guard. It was not until 2005, with the rise of the Pistons on one end and Steve Nash's Suns on the other end, that managers fully realized that building around a shoot-first guard is not as easy as Jordan made it seem. Perhaps if Philadelphia's managers had realized this sooner, they would have done a better job building around Iverson. Iverson represented the era of iso-ball that dominated the early 2000s better than anyone else. But the fact that he dominated is less his fault and more that of managers who were trapped by Jordan's legend and proved to be unable to think of a new creative strategy.

Chapter 10: Iverson's Legacy and Future

Aristotle once said of tragedies that their hero must have a flaw, which ultimately brings about their downfall. Under those conditions, Iverson is, in a sense, a tragic hero. His career ended on a low note, playing for a 76ers team that signed him up more to sell tickets than to play winning basketball. He was brought down by repeatedly clashing with the coaching staff and management of Detroit and Memphis, refusing to lower himself to the level of a role player and refusing to acknowledge that he was no longer at the level that he was in the past. His pride and refusal to accept the present took him out of the NBA.

However, does Iverson see himself that way? Does he look back at his career with regret? Does he think how he failed to win a championship and how his career ended so badly? Does he think of how he lingered around a ghost at the fringes of the NBA for a chance to return – a chance that never came? Iverson stated that he does not. He said that he has no regrets about anything in his career – how it ended, how he failed to win a title, not even the "practice" rant that was replayed endlessly by the media. Early in his career, he told the media, *"I don't want to be like Michael. I don't want to be like Magic. I don't want to be like Bird or Isaiah. When my career's over, I want to look in the mirror and know that I did it my way."*

Iverson did do it his way. He played his way, a style of basketball that made coaches tear their hair out. However, it was a style that led the Philadelphia 76ers to the NBA Finals. Some even perceive Iverson's style as arrogant, as a refusal to conform to the rules and the team. When he was with the 2004 USA Olympic Team, his only appearance at the Olympics, collapsed and shocked the world by earning only a bronze medal, journalists who knew nothing about sports wrung their hands and contrasted American "selfish" basketball with the "team-orientated" style of international players. Iverson was implicitly and explicitly the target of such criticisms. No one bothered to mention that while so many NBA stars like Kobe Bryant, Tracy McGrady, and Shaquille O'Neal decided not to go to the Olympics. Iverson was there for his country – the same country that, at one point, had tossed him in prison. In the eyes of his critics, he was still an arrogant, selfish player.

However, for others, Iverson was not just a great basketball player. He was an inspiration. He was a model of how a little guy, with enough work and will, could accomplish things that absolutely no one had expected him to achieve. Iverson may not be the best player of his era, but everyone wanted to be like him.

He was able to put up impressive numbers for the majority of his NBA career despite not being the tallest or the biggest. He was a real inspiration for anyone who felt they might be too small to make it to the big leagues.

Aristotle may have said that a man brought down by his path is a tragic hero, but he also said that a tragedy must inspire *pathos*, or pity, in its audience. In the case of Iverson, however, he inspired awe. Perhaps, that makes him not a tragic hero, but a hero that anyone that identifies with him could admire.

Final Word/About the Author

I was born and raised in Norwalk, Connecticut. Growing up, I could often be found spending many nights watching basketball, soccer, and football matches with my father in the family living room. I love sports and everything that sports can embody. I believe that sports are one of most genuine forms of competition, heart, and determination. I write my works to learn more about influential athletes in the hopes that from my writing, you the reader can walk away inspired to put in an equal if not greater amount of hard work and perseverance to pursue your goals. If you enjoyed *Allen Iverson: The Inspiring Story of One of Basketball's Greatest Shooting Guards,* please leave a review! Also, you can read more of my works on *Andrew Luck, Rob Gronkowski, Brett Favre, Calvin Johnson, Drew Brees, J.J. Watt, Colin Kaepernick, Aaron Rodgers, Peyton Manning, Tom Brady, Russell Wilson, Michael Jordan, LeBron James, Kyrie Irving, Klay Thompson, Stephen Curry, Kevin Durant, Russell Westbrook, Anthony Davis, Chris Paul, Blake Griffin, Kobe Bryant, Joakim Noah, Scottie Pippen, Carmelo Anthony, Kevin Love, Grant Hill, Tracy McGrady, Vince Carter, Patrick Ewing, Karl Malone, Tony Parker, Hakeem Olajuwon, Reggie Miller, Michael Carter-Williams, John Wall, James Harden, Tim Duncan, Steve Nash, Draymond Green, Kawhi Leonard,*

Dwyane Wade, Ray Allen, Pau Gasol, Dirk Nowitzki, Jimmy Butler, Paul Pierce, Manu Ginobili, Pete Maravich, Larry Bird, Kyle Lowry, Jason Kidd, David Robinson, LaMarcus Aldridge, Derrick Rose, Paul George, Kevin Garnett, Chris Paul, Marc Gasol, Yao Ming and Al Horford in the Kindle Store. If you love basketball, check out my website at claytongeoffreys.com to join my exclusive list where I let you know about my latest books and give you lots of goodies.

Like what you read? Please leave a review!

I write because I love sharing the stories of influential people like Allen Iverson with fantastic readers like you. My readers inspire me to write more so please do not hesitate to let me know what you thought by leaving a review! If you love books on life, basketball, or productivity, check out my website at claytongeoffreys.com to join my exclusive list where I let you know about my latest books. Aside from being the first to hear about my latest releases, you can also download a free copy of *33 Life Lessons: Success Principles, Career Advice & Habits of Successful People*. See you there!

Clayton

References

[i] Walks, Matt. "Allen Iverson's Practice Rant: What Has Been Forgotten 14 Years Late". *ESPN*. 10 September 2015. Web.
[ii] Begley, Ian. "Allen Iverson, Kenyon Martin Among Former NBA Players To Join 3-On-3 League". *ESPN*. 18 February 2017.

Made in the USA
Middletown, DE
29 July 2019